THE
CIVIL WAR
— ALONG —
TENNESSEE'S
CUMBERLAND
PLATEAU

AARON ASTOR

THE
History
PRESS

Published by The History Press
Charleston, SC 29403
www.historypress.net

Images are courtesy of the author unless otherwise noted.

Cover image: *Battle of Lookout Mountain* by James Walker. *Courtesy of the Tennessee State Library and Archives.*

First published 2015

ISBN 978-1-5402-0984-9

Library of Congress Control Number: 2015932376

Notice: The information in this book is true and complete to the best of our knowledge. It is offered without guarantee on the part of the authors or The History Press. The authors and The History Press disclaim all liability in connection with the use of this book.

CONTENTS

PREFACE

After the panels concluded at the Tennessee Preservation Trust Conference in Cookeville in May 2013, a whole group of us piled into a van and set out to the green rolling hills of White County. Among us were some of the premier experts on the history of the Upper Cumberland region, including Tennessee Tech's Calvin Dickinson, Michael "Birdie" Birdwell and Kent Dollar, as well as Brian McKnight, Mark Dudney and several other historians and preservationists. This was an unusual tour through an unusual area. We stopped at cemeteries with strange comb graves, a church that was attacked during the Civil War, a massacre site called Dug Hill, the grave of Champ Ferguson and the Sparta cemetery where General George Dibrell was buried. Afterward, we approached what looked like an ordinary farm in a wooded country lot and pulled in. It was no ordinary farm. It was the Calfkiller Brewery. Needless to say, this region hooked me like no other.

It wasn't the first time I'd gone exploring in this part of the state. Just about every other weekend over the last two years, I have had the chance to take my two sons Henry and Teddy, and often my dad, on hiking adventures to some previously unknown (to us at least) place on the Cumberland Plateau. Living so close to Great Smoky Mountains National Park, it seems a bit indulgent to go all the way to the other side of the great valley for hiking and exploring, but such is the attraction of the plateau for all of us. The waterfalls, caves, rock houses and arches are sources of never-ending wonder and adventure around the house.

PREFACE

After writing several articles for the *New York Times* Disunion series on Civil War Tennessee and giving multiple presentations to historical and genealogical groups about divided loyalties in Tennessee, I decided it was time to do a book project on the state I've called home since 2007. And after getting Birdie's encouragement, I decided to take on the Civil War along Tennessee's Cumberland Plateau. The opportunity to combine a passion for Civil War history and the wildness of Tennessee's lush Cumberland Plateau was too much to pass up.

Several people were especially helpful in making this book a reality. Kirsten Schofield, former commissioning editor at The History Press, first suggested a book of this kind, and I thank her for the opportunity. Birdie provided me with a thorough 290-page bibliography of the Cumberland Plateau that is a scholar's dream. James Jones at the Tennessee Historical Commission generously provided me with an edited portion of the Tennessee Civil War Sourcebook focusing on the plateau. Mark Dudney alerted me to much of the story in White County, including his mother's fine master's thesis on the Civil War in White County. Karen Beaty Eldridge, director of marketing at Maryville College (MC) and a native of Scott County, put me in contact with her aunt Martha Wiley and Fentress County historian Willie Beaty. Much of what I was able to discover about Fentress County was through the amazing local history and genealogy work in Jamestown. Former and current Maryville College students of mine from Scott County, including Josh Terry, Afton Boles and Craig Owens, were instrumental in stoking my interest in the area around the Big South Fork. The amazing work of students and staff at the Museum of Scott County at Scott High School shows that local history is in good hands on the Cumberland Plateau. Other students of mine living along the plateau have been equally helpful in bringing my attention to local stories, including Adam Moore, Lindsay O'Neal, Emily Boren and Shelby Gunn.

At Cumberland Gap National Historical Park, rangers Scott Teodorski and Pam Eddy have generously taken my MC students through the gap and explained the pioneer and Civil War history there. Dot Kelly of the Knoxville Civil War Roundtable has done some great research on William P. Sanders's 1863 raid, and Joan Markel has shared her expertise on Ambrose Burnside's path through the Cumberlands to Knoxville. Mark Stanfill, Judy Varner, Bob Fulcher and many others have been working tirelessly to build and preserve the natural and cultural history of the Cumberland Trail along the plateau. College students on spring "breakaway" building the trail and learning about the region are making it possible for future generations to keep this story alive. It was a distinct pleasure to share the Civil War story with students from my alma mater, Hamilton College, while they were staying at Soddy-Daisy on an alternative spring break.

Brian McKnight has generously shared some of his research on Champ Ferguson, beyond what already appears in his excellent book. Jim Ogden of Chickamauga-Chattanooga National Military Park and Anthony Hodges, a fellow board member of the Tennessee Civil War Preservation Association, were extremely helpful in explaining the topography of the ridges around Chattanooga and the lower Sequatchie Valley. Merritt Blakeslee was very helpful in sharing his research on the Civil War at Sewanee, as was John Willis. Jay Clark, a great singer-songwriter/wildlife biologist/colleague at MC, generously shared his knowledge of Franklin County, Peter Turney and the Cowan Tunnel. My MC colleague Paul Threadgill helped me to understand the intersection of geology and botany on the plateau and in Tennessee in general. Mary Ann Peckham, executive director of the Tennessee Civil War Preservation Association, has helped stoke my interest in this project, especially as it relates to the preservation of historic sites across the state. Minoa Uffelman, Carole Bucy, Scott MacKenzie, Bob Hutton, J. Michael Rhyne, Mark Banker, William Hardy, Stephen Ash, Keri Leigh Merritt, Susan O'Donovan, Jonathan Sarris, Cherel Henderson, Steve Cotham, John Inscoe, Barton Myers, Kenneth Noe, Gordon Belt, Ann Toplovich, Sam Elliott, Steve Dean, George Lane and Fred Prouty have all inspired me with their love of Tennessee, Appalachian and southern history. And thanks to the late Michael Fellman, a true mentor of mine who taught so many of us about the true meaning of war and peace.

I also want to thank my family for putting up with random interjections about the Cumberland Plateau. The love and support from my mother and father, Ronnie and Mark Astor, and my sister, Rachel, and her husband, Scot, are beyond measure. My sons Henry and Teddy have been enthusiastic hiking companions and have braved bees, stinging nettles and perilous rock faces with me. Finally, I want to thank my lovely wife, Samantha, for her support and patience as I put this book together. Since beginning the project, we have been fortunate to add three new bundles of joy to our family: Jimmy, born in December 2013, and our twin girls, Sadie and Lillian, born just before Christmas 2014. This book is dedicated to them.

INTRODUCTION

In late September 1861, a band of Confederate soldiers in northern Fentress County, under the command of Captain W. Scott Bledsoe, "dashed over the line" into Kentucky. Bledsoe hoped to "free" several pro-Confederate citizens being harassed by "Lincoln men" in Albany, Kentucky. After fighting off a local Unionist Home Guard, Bledsoe captured dozens of guns and supplies and returned to Tennessee. Hearing of the raid, Home Guards from neighboring counties flocked to Albany and vowed revenge against the Confederate Tennesseans and their "traitorous" Kentucky allies. Learning of a makeshift encampment at a place called Travisville, just thirteen miles from Albany, these Union Home Guards, along with several regular Federal soldiers, set out to recover their stolen arms and break up the Rebel rendezvous. Captain Morrison of Company C in the First Kentucky Cavalry Regiment (USA) organized a scouting expedition with fellow cavalrymen and several members of the Hustonville Home Guard.[1] Morrison's men surprised the Travisville camp, killed a man named James Saufley, took a few prisoners and scattered the rest of the Rebels.[2] With the so-called Affair at Travisville, the deadly Civil War had arrived on the Cumberland Plateau and in the state of Tennessee.

Though a minor engagement that has largely escaped the attention of historians, the Affair at Travisville marked the first Civil War military engagement in Tennessee. The small-scale, guerrilla-style raid by mixed forces of enlisted soldiers and ad hoc militiamen, many of them kin to one another, foreshadowed the kind of fighting that would take place

Site of the "Travisville Affair," the first military action in Tennessee during the
Civil War. James Saufley, killed in the battle, is buried in this cemetery.

throughout the Cumberland Plateau region during the Civil War. Among
the Unionist raiders at Travisville—and the likely gunman who killed
Saufley—was Jim Ferguson of Clinton County, Kentucky.[3] His better-known
brother, Champ Ferguson, the most notorious Confederate guerrilla of the
entire region, was among the Confederate troops near Travisville. The Civil
War on the Cumberland Plateau was a family affair, a desperate and deadly
scuffle that never seemed to end and a key battlefront for resources and
pathways into Unionist Kentucky and Confederate Georgia and Alabama.
Amanda McDowell, a Unionist woman in mostly pro-Confederate White

County, confided to her diary a sense of fear, confusion and despair shared by most of her neighbors.[4] Making matters worse, her beloved brother Fayette enthusiastically joined the Confederate army, forcing her to choose between her dedication to the Union and her brother's well-being. In her household, her community, her state and her country, she was caught in between. As her grandniece described it, she was truly in "No Man's Land."[5]

But if McDowell suffered the privations of guerrilla war in the relative obscurity of the Calfkiller River Valley and the dozens of men skirmishing in the Wolf River area around Travisville caught the attention of few, tens of thousands of other soldiers would find themselves fighting near one of the most heavily photographed battlegrounds in American history: Lookout Mountain, just south of the city of Chattanooga. Meanwhile, to the north and east of McDowell's White County, the famous Cumberland Gap beckoned large armies anxious to choke off enemy invasion. That natural pathway, denuded of all its trees, stood out to Civil War generals on both sides as a key transit route between Unionist Kentucky and Confederate Tennessee. Both Lookout Mountain and Cumberland Gap underscore the strategic importance of the Cumberland Plateau for more conventional military activity. The plateau experienced warfare both large and small, and not a man, woman or child, free or enslaved, could escape its devastation.

Tennessee's Cumberland Plateau is a physiographic region of stunning beauty, imposing rock faces, geologic oddities and paradoxical importance in the geography of Tennessee. From the early nineteenth century onward, Tennesseans spoke of three "Grand Divisions"—East, Middle and West—each with its own physical features, economic systems and political and cultural makeups. The Cumberland Plateau makes a boundary between the East and Middle divisions, containing within it elements of both. The modern time zone boundary between eastern and central time bisects the plateau, laying down an extra artificial division to further complicate the identity of the plateau. Nevertheless, it is clear to any observer that the Cumberland Plateau is an actual, distinctive geomorphic region with a continuous elevation along the rim at around 1,800 feet. It is also a region that experienced a war that both resembled the kind of internecine conflict found elsewhere in Appalachia and resembled nothing else at all.

This book serves a couple of main purposes. First, it offers to general readers an introduction to the Civil War experience along Tennessee's Cumberland Plateau. Longtime inhabitants of the plateau, recent arrivals, tourists visiting its many beautiful parks and forests, Tennesseans curious about the Civil War era and general Civil War readers will hopefully find much to interest them in this book.

Another purpose is to pursue some newer conceptual approaches to Civil War history. First, the book places the Civil War experience in the context of much deeper geological and ecological forces, thus contributing to a newer subfield known as "Big History."[6] The multilayered, interlocking geology of the plateau is more than a metaphor for the Civil War. It is also a very real foundation for human settlement, movement and conflict. Viewing the recent human history of the Cumberland Plateau in light of this much larger natural history places the Civil War in a deeper geospatial context.

Second, this book employs research tools that make possible a more thorough reading of nineteenth-century rural communities and the social networks among them than was possible in the past. Historians have used genealogical tools like census records, deeds and military service records for decades, but the digitization of these records has allowed for deeper analysis of spatial, socioeconomic and kinship trends and over a wider expanse than simply one or two counties.

Third, the book contributes in small but vital ways to our understanding of guerrilla conflict, a subfield of Civil War studies and one that has garnered significant interest in recent years. This is especially true for the study of Unionist guerrilla organizations like the Independent Scouts under Tinker Dave Beaty's command, which have remained largely understudied up to now. Confederate guerrillas in Missouri, Kentucky, Tennessee, Virginia and elsewhere have rightly received great scholarly attention in recent years. But the Unionist guerrillas, some of them given official Federal commands and some not, also demand serious study.

Fourth, *The Civil War Along Tennessee's Cumberland Plateau* sheds light on the personal and cultural geography of the residents who lived on the plateau and the soldiers and officers who navigated their way across a very complex topography. Much of the Civil War experience on the plateau was determined by what people knew to be "over there," beyond circumscribed spatial boundaries, and what they did not know about enemy troop movements, guerrilla marauders, passable gaps and valleys and the loyalty and hospitality of strangers.

And finally, by focusing on the people who lived along the Cumberland Plateau before, during and after the Civil War, the book gives insight into how these communities changed after years of destructive war and how various longtime residents and new arrivals envisioned a post–Civil War society.

INTRODUCTION

The chapters in this book are organized both thematically and chronologically. The first outlines the geographic contours of the plateau, as well as the complex geologic process through which the plateau came into being. The second chapter explores the settlement of people along the plateau, right up to 1861 and the outbreak of hostilities. Chapter 3 focuses on the secession crisis and the outbreak of war, with particular emphasis on divided loyalties in the region. The fourth chapter examines the conventional war raging across the Cumberland Plateau, especially in 1862 and 1863. Chapter 5 addresses the guerrilla conflict that engulfed the region early on and never abated until after April 1865. And the final chapter considers the process of Reconstruction on the Cumberland Plateau and what that entailed.

1

THE CUMBERLAND PLATEAU IN SPACE AND TIME

In 1876, the Tennessee Bureau of Agriculture, Statistics and Mines published a "collection of facts" regarding the state's "agricultural and mineral wealth." After highlighting the luxuriant and fertile soils of the valley of East Tennessee, the tract described the "Cumberland Table-land" to the west, a "high-elevated plateau, that rises in massive grandeur to an average elevation of 2,000 feet above the sea, and 1,000 feet above the Valley."[1] Though "the soil of this division is sandy, thin, porous and unproductive, and it is of but little agricultural importance," the plateau maintained, "buried in its bosom…huge treasures of coal and iron." Bordered on the east by a ridge that "rises with abruptness that is marked and striking," the western edge is, by contrast, "irregular and jagged, notched and scalloped by deep coves and valleys, which are separated by finger-like spurs."

The Cumberland Plateau presented a geographic paradox to settlers and prospectors of the nineteenth century, just as it did to officers and soldiers tasked with controlling the region during the Civil War. The plateau is at times flat and wide open, with grasses perfect for livestock to roam freely. A physician from Chattanooga commented in an 1885 supplement to *Scientific American*, "The whole Cumberland table, with the exception of that small part which is under cultivation, is one great free, open pasture for all the cattle of the valleys."[2] The flatness is deceiving, however, as innocent lines of trees in the distance typically signal the presence of a massive rupture in the earth's surface. One of those, possibly named by the famed Tennessean David Crockett, is the Fiery Gizzard. Beginning as

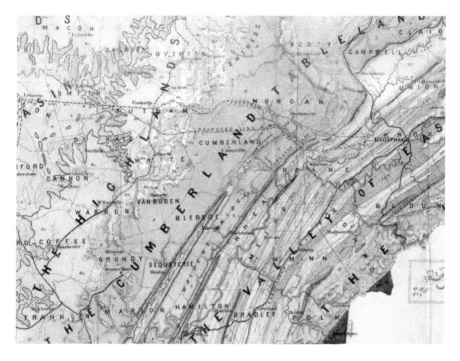

This "Geological Map of Tennessee" accompanied James Safford's 1869 book titled *The Geology of Tennessee. Courtesy of the Harold B. Lee Library at Brigham Young University.*

a quiet stream in the Grundy County town of Tracy City, the Fiery Gizzard Creek slices through the sandstone caprock to reach the softer limestone and shale layers beneath.[3] Gravity carries the Fiery Gizzard over waterfalls and past rock chimneys, boulder gardens and rock houses through one of the lushest gorges in North America. Wildflowers and rare plants cover the gorge floor throughout the year. At the bottom of the mountain, the Fiery Gizzard joins another picturesque creek emerging from Sweedens Cove to form Battle Creek, which flows into the Tennessee River Gorge near the current city of South Pittsburg. Westbound travelers on Interstate 24 today notice the dramatic scenery of Fiery Gizzard Cove as they wind their way up Monteagle Mountain toward Nashville.[4]

Few places in the eastern United States boast the geological peculiarity, topographic complexity and biological diversity of the Cumberland Plateau. A combination of Utah-style rock formations and lush gorges, waterfalls and forested rims, the Cumberland Plateau showcases some of the most unusual landscape in the Northern Hemisphere. It is also the longest hardwood forest plateau in the world. The Cumberland Plateau is but a sliver of a larger geographic entity, the Appalachian Plateau, which is itself a province of the Appalachian Mountain system. Vast as the system is, smaller geologic zones in the "deep coves and valleys" have created microclimates and patches of fertile soil that would profoundly affect patterns of human settlement.

This chapter explores the Cumberland Plateau in space and time. The purpose is not simply to draw a portrait of the region and its natural development but to demonstrate how later human settlement, and human conflict, occurred within the natural framework laid out over hundreds of millions of years. The plateau's landscape was perfect for guerrilla war, with gaps and ridges perfectly located to shield troop movements and provide cover for ambushes and hit-and-run attacks. Meanwhile, hollows formed by erosion encouraged pockets of settlement that linked inhabitants to the outside world through tight river valleys. These zones of semi-isolation forced communities to rely more on one another for survival than in most other sections of antebellum America. But it also encouraged the development of certain kinds of social networks among plateau residents and between certain plateau elites and the outside world. These networks would go a long way toward accounting for divided loyalties during the Civil War. The landscape was marked by time for close-knit survival and for bitter internecine war.

The relationship between the land and the people at war is metaphoric, too. The layering of hard rock strata, punctured by deep gorges, with occasional rock windows and waterfalls as evidence of the uneven process of erosion, embodies the jagged border characteristic of the Cumberland Plateau at war. Peoples who mixed freely with one another for decades suddenly discovered that small fault lines within their communities opened up into deep ravines, valleys and "gulfs" of conflict and chaos. Literally and figuratively, fault lines of loyalty between Union and Confederate sympathizers traced the fractures, joints and faults in the plateau's sandstone caprock.

It is first necessary to outline precisely where the Cumberland Plateau is as a geographic entity. We will then discuss the peculiarities of the landscape within Tennessee's Cumberland Plateau. Following this review of the geography is a broad geologic overview of the plateau's formation. Finally, we address the appearance of natural and human life up to the time of the first permanent European settlers in the late eighteenth century.

The Southern Appalachian Mountain system contains several geographic "provinces," each with distinctive characteristics and similar geology.[5] From the Atlantic coast to the west, the first province after leaving the coastal plain is the Piedmont, or foothills region. A noticeable "fall line" separates

Layers of sandstone at Rock Island along the Caney Fork River.

the Piedmont from the Coastal Plain, and much of the great population settlement of the East Coast occurs near the fall line. Cities like New York, Philadelphia, Baltimore, Washington and Richmond emerged just below this long fall line, beyond which ships could no longer travel with ease.

To the west of the Piedmont is the Blue Ridge, a long succession of high ridges that surpass six thousand feet at several points. The Blue Ridge reaches the highest elevation of the Appalachian chain, especially in North Carolina and Tennessee. At times a narrow ridgeline in Virginia and at others a maze of transverse mountains like the majestic Black, Balsam and Great Smokies, the Blue Ridge marks the eastern edge of the Appalachian chain.[6]

Beyond the Blue Ridge lies the Valley and Ridge Province, which includes a series of parallel ridges of different sizes in a corduroy-like pattern. Erosion from major rivers would broaden these valleys out, flattening some of the lower ridges and creating spillways for smaller creeks. Rivers drain the Valley and Ridge Province in a trellis-like pattern, with long parallel courses on a northeast-southwest axis followed by brief right-angle turns.[7] At some points, this would take the form of a Great Valley, such as the Shenandoah and the Tennessee, where soil was most fertile and settlement was greatest.

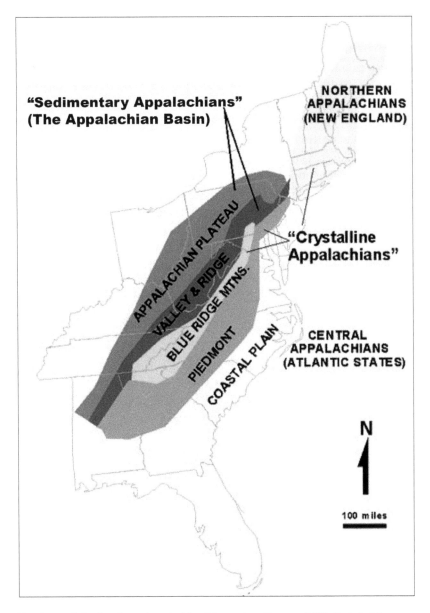

Provinces of the Southern Appalachian Mountains. *Courtesy of U.S. Geological Survey.*

The Blue Ridge and Valley and Ridge Provinces continue from southern Pennsylvania to Georgia.

To the west of the Valley and Ridge Province is the Appalachian Plateau. On the eastern edge of the plateau is an abrupt escarpment, very difficult to ascend or cross at many points. Called Walden Ridge or Cumberland Mountain in most of Tennessee, and Allegheny Mountain in West Virginia, this sharp ridge demarcates a very different geomorphic and geologic zone than the valley. Instead of a continuing series of parallel ridges, or a downward slope to the west of the great escarpment, the landscape takes the form of an elevated tableland—a plateau. It begins in Alabama and continues as far north as New York State. But the plateau is rarely flat. At some points, like in Campbell, Anderson and Morgan Counties, a group of larger mountains appears on top of the plateau. Elsewhere, the plateau is deeply eroded or "dissected" by creeks that cut through the sandstone caprock and eat away at the softer limestone and shale vlayers beneath.[8]

Cumberland Plateau is part of the Appalachian Plateau Province. *Courtesy of Imus Geographics.*

Generally speaking, the Appalachian Plateau is divided into two regions, each named for the main river system that originates within it. The Allegheny Plateau, at the north, drains both the Allegheny and Monongahela River watersheds that form the Ohio River at Pittsburgh. The Cumberland Plateau begins in eastern Kentucky at the headwaters of the Cumberland River but also includes many creeks that drain into the Tennessee River. Most of the Cumberland Plateau lies in Tennessee, where it stretches for fifty-five miles along the Kentucky border and thirty-eight miles along the border with Alabama.[9]

This book is titled "The Civil War *Along* Tennessee's Cumberland Plateau" for an important reason. The geological features and population settlements immediately "off" the plateau affected events on the plateau and vice versa. To the west of the Appalachian Plateau is a rolling terrain, characterized in some places by karst and caves and in other places by relatively flat, fertile land. In Tennessee, the region to the west of the Cumberland Plateau is known as the Highland Rim, as it surrounds the Nashville Basin and occupies an elevation point midway between the plateau and the basin. In many places, it is known as the Plateau of the Barrens, as its cherty soil makes for poor cultivation.[10] More important than the elevation difference between the Highland Rim and Cumberland Plateau is the "jagged and irregular" nature of the dividing line between the two. Some of the most spectacular landforms in Tennessee, including Fall Creek Falls and Pogue Creek Canyon, are carved into this western edge of the plateau. During the Civil War, the most notorious guerrillas operated along the rivers and creeks emerging from the plateau's western slope. The rock crevices, caves and narrow beds of the Calfkiller, Wolf, Obey, Collins and Caney Fork Rivers sheltered many of these guerrillas, as well as civilians hiding from them.

West of the Highland Rim in Tennessee is the agricultural heartland of the Nashville Basin. The Cumberland River flows down from Kentucky and into the Nashville Basin before turning back north to the Ohio River. Surprisingly, the Nashville Basin was originally a dome that protruded through resistant sandstone.[11] It eroded to a point lower than the surrounding Highland Rim during the Ordovician period (more than 444 million years ago), leaving a fertile, limestone-rich soil at its base. The basin is shaped like a vertical oval, stretching as far south as Giles County, though it is not as wide from east to west. The fertile farmland, turnpike and railroad networks and political power emanating from the state capital made the Nashville Basin the most important geomorphic region in the state during the Civil War.[12] Political, trade and social networks between the plateau and the Nashville

Pogue Creek Canyon in current Pickett County, formerly Fentress County. Wind erosion produces arches, windows and "holes" in the rock.

Basin would help determine patterns of loyalty and military enlistment from the earliest days of the Civil War to the end.

The variegated terrain on the plateau itself requires further explanation, as its features would play an important role in the Civil War. Going from the northeast to the southwest, the first feature of note is Cumberland Gap at the northeastern extremity of Tennessee's Cumberland Plateau.[13] The entire eastern escarpment of the plateau in the northern part of the state is known as Cumberland Mountain. As with other sections of the eastern escarpment, human passage over the mountain was possible only at certain "gaps" or low points along the ridge. Cumberland Gap was, by far, the largest and most navigable passageway over Cumberland Mountain. It was made even more important due to the presence of a parallel gap in Pine Mountain twelve miles to the north in Kentucky at a place called the Narrows. The river carving the Narrows was the actual Cumberland River, making its way down from the mountains of southeastern Kentucky. These twin gaps beckoned hundreds of thousands of migrants on their passage into the West around the turn of the nineteenth century.[14]

Springs along the top of Cumberland Mountain occasionally eroded the ridgeline to form smaller gaps. The next navigable gap appears where Big Creek cut a passage through the mountain near the current town of LaFollette. At the western edge of Cumberland Mountain is Wheelers Gap, the future site of Caryville and Bruce's Gap, where Interstate 75 passes through. Devil's Racetrack, a series of vertical rock chimneys resembling teeth, appears just north of here. The broken sandstone columns are a result of tectonic pressure whose origin will be described shortly. The pressure compressed and folded the horizontal rock layers until they became vertical and then snapped. Subsequent erosion of the softer Chattanooga shale beds left behind a hard sandstone quartz conglomerate that remains as the Devil's Racetrack.[15] The tectonic pressure managed to shift the entire rectangular series of rocks—the Cumberland Block—ten miles to the northwest, along what geologists call the Pine Mountain Overthrust Fault.[16] The Elk Fork Creek forms at the southwestern edge of the Cumberland Block and heads to the northeast, making a perfect course for the parallel Interstate 75. In fact, Interstate 75, like earlier rail and turnpike routes, followed the zigzag path created by tectonic forces more than 250 million years ago.

The same tectonic pressure created a series of transverse mountains just beyond Devil's Racetrack. This area, stretching northeastward into eastern Kentucky, is generally referred to as the Cumberland Mountains because of its appearance atop the already elevated Cumberland Plateau. It begins at a fault line near the Emory River and rests atop the so-called Wartburg Basin, known especially for its rich sources of coal underneath.[17] This high-elevation section continues northeastward to the Jacksboro Fault, where the Cumberland Block begins and the transverse mountains shift to the northwest. This section includes Cross Mountain, the highest point west of the Smokies until reaching South Dakota. Several other mountains within the so-called Cumberland Mountains pierce the sky nearby, including Pine Mountain (parallel to Cumberland Mountain), Jellico Mountain, Bird

The Cumberland Mountains, including Frozen Head Peak, are like a "pile of books on a table." The plateau flattens out to the west toward Wartburg.

Mountain (in Frozen Head State Park), Smoky Mountain (not to be confused with the Great Smoky Mountains), Pilot Mountain, Big Brushy Mountain and, at the southwestern extremity, the Crab Orchard Mountains. These mountains, exceeding three thousand feet in elevation, are described by geologist Edward Luther as like "a pile of books" atop the plateau "table" and include terrain so rugged that they are still mostly unsettled.[18] However, they also contained "in their bosom" the majority of the region's coal resources and would be the site of some of the nation's most dramatic labor struggles in the late nineteenth century.

West of this collection of higher mountains is the Cumberland Plateau proper, where it flattens out into Scott, Morgan, Cumberland and Fentress Counties. Rivers like the New, Obed, Emory and the Big South Fork of the Cumberland River repeatedly dissect the flat sections of the plateau, creating spectacular gorges flanked by sandstone cliffs several hundred feet above the river floor. Smaller creeks, like Daddy's and Mammy's Creeks in Cumberland County and Brimstone, Buffalo and Clear Fork Creeks in Scott County, also carve impressive channels into the plateau surface as they make their way into larger waterways.[19] The erosion-resistant sandstone caprock forces these creeks to make many twists and turns before reaching the bottom. In the bends of these twists are "hollows" or "flats" with relatively habitable land for settlement. In the middle of the plateau lies the Tennessee Valley Divide; waterways to the south and east of the divide flow into the Tennessee River (often via the Clinch or Emory Rivers), while those to the north and west join the Cumberland River watershed.

Along the western slope are creeks and rivers that form wider coves and hollows in the plateau. They carve out the "irregular and jagged" border between the Cumberland Plateau and the Highland Rim and make for some of the most fertile farmland in the area. Most of them flow into the Cumberland River, including the Wolf River and East Fork of the Obey River in Fentress County; the Caney Fork River in Cumberland, White, Warren and DeKalb Counties; the Calfkiller River and Falling Water River in White County; the Rocky River in Van Buren County; and the Collins River in Grundy and Warren County. Piney, Cane and Fall Creeks in Van Buren County drain into the Caney Fork after tumbling over magnificent waterfalls within the current Fall Creek Falls State Park. To the southwest flows the Elk River from Grundy County and Boiling Fork Creek in Franklin County. Some creeks along the southern plateau—like Richland Creek in Rhea County; the Fiery Gizzard in Grundy and Marion Counties; the Sequatchie River through Bledsoe, Sequatchie and Marion Counties; and Battle Creek in Marion County—run into the Tennessee River.

Water is the most powerful erosive force in nature, and the precise topography along the Cumberland Plateau is, to a large extent, the result of water erosion. Where water has eroded the sandstone plateau surface, it typically creates very deep impressions in the earth because the carbonate layers underneath are much softer and more susceptible to erosion. As the erosion continues, the gorges become wider, forming "coves"—small

Layers of sandstone, shale and limestone in the Fiery Gizzard Gorge.

valleys encased by mountains on all sides—revealing rich organic soil fit for cultivation and settlement. The wealthiest farmers and merchants tended to live in these coves, and they exploited the river systems to ship agricultural produce and livestock to wider markets.

Water also shaped the subterranean world, especially in the karst lands west of the plateau. Geologists and cavers estimate that there are as many as 1,169 caves in White County alone, with 836 in Van Buren County.[20] Fentress, Overton, Putnam and Marion Counties each have more than 500 known caves, and Warren and Franklin have more than 400. In addition to caves are sinkholes, some of them so massive as to produce a "cove." The junction of several sinkholes in the plateau surface formed Grassy Cove in Cumberland County.[21] A creek passing into Mill Cave at the south end of Grassy Cove emerges several miles to the south as the headwaters of the Sequatchie River. Caves were especially important in the Civil War era because of the presence of saltpeter, or potassium nitrate. Saltpeter is a key ingredient in the production of gunpowder; decades before the Civil War, gunpowder manufacturers from as far away as Delaware purchased saltpeter mined in caves near the Cumberland Plateau. Especially important sources of saltpeter during the Civil War were Saltpeter Cave in Grassy Cove; Fultz Saltpeter Cave in Grundy County; Lookout Mountain Cave in Hamilton County; Nickajack and Monteagle Saltpeter Caves in Marion County; Johnson and Calfkiller Saltpeter Caves in Putnam County; Big Bone Cave in Van Buren County; Hubbard, Little Bat and Cumberland Caverns in Warren County; and the Cave Hill Saltpeter Pits in White County.[22] When these caves were inaccessible to the Confederate army in the latter half of the Civil War, the Nitre and Mining Bureau turned to caves in northeast Alabama and northwest Georgia (also part of the Cumberland Plateau).[23]

Air and wind also eroded much of the plateau surface. As with water erosion, air erosion affects different rock types in different ways. Sandstone caprock resists both water and wind erosion, but the softer shale and limestone underneath eroded nonetheless. The result is the creation of arches, windows, rock chimneys and rock houses, especially along the ledges and rims of the plateau.[24] Twin Arches near the Big South Fork is arguably the largest set of natural bridges in the eastern United States. Tom Dunigan, a geographer at the University of Tennessee, has identified as many as sixty arches in Fentress County alone.[25] Rock houses occasionally contained saltpeter as well, though they were most useful during the Civil War as hiding places for deserters, guerrillas and civilians.

The most noteworthy indentation in the plateau is the Sequatchie Valley. A perfectly straight and narrow valley with fertile fields up and down, the Sequatchie is one of the most picturesque places in Tennessee.[26] The valley is sixty-five miles long from the head of the Sequatchie River to the Alabama state line, where it continues for eighty more miles as Browns Valley. Though scientists long thought it was formed as a rift valley, geologists have concluded that the Sequatchie is actually an anticline, an upward fold of stratified rocks created by a thrust fault. The folded sandstone arched and cracked and then eroded, leaving an unusually fertile strip of land that would attract foragers from both armies during the Civil War.[27]

So how did the Cumberland Plateau form? What accounts for its size and distinctive characteristics? How have geologists explained the origin of the Cumberland Plateau over time? To study the geology of the Cumberland Plateau is to study its deep history going back hundreds of millions of years before human life appeared. Geologists have examined the molecular framework of rocks, the order of rock strata, rock deformations on the landscape and the exposed outcroppings of unusual rock patterns to draw conclusions about the formation of the Cumberland Plateau.

One of the most remarkable things about geology is how recently its unifying governing theory—plate tectonics—has emerged.[28] Only in the 1960s, with the discovery of the Mid-Atlantic Rift and sea floor spreading, did geologists begin to understand how crust on the earth's surface moved—or that it moved at all. Though the mechanism of plate tectonics was understood only recently, many core elements of geology have been known for much longer, including the age of rock formations. When James Hutton, the Scottish father of modern geology, began his explorations into the formation of the earth's surface, he and his successors developed a few important principles. First, the present is the key to understanding the past. Laws of geology rarely (if ever) change, so the same kinds of geologic forces at work today can be assumed to have occurred in the past. Since many of these geologic forces, like erosion, occur at a very slow rate, it stands to reason that the earth is likely more than four billion years old, and the formation of the features of the earth's crust must be understood in "deep time" over hundreds of millions of years.[29]

Hutton and his successors developed a typology of rock types and a chronology of their formation based on a few other key principles. Sediment forms in layers, so without any further deformation, deeper rocks in the surface are older than those close to the surface. Also, elements tend to decay at a constant rate. So the rate of decay of certain elements within a particular rock formation can be used as a "decoder" for measuring the age of the overall rock. Later geologists would turn to uranium isotopes as the best measuring stick for the age of the earth's rocks. With these tools at their disposal, Hutton's followers (most of them in Great Britain) began to catalogue, name and date various rock formations found around the world. The name and dating system is still used for the most part today.

Traditionally, geologists divided time based on the earliest known presence of life forms, roughly 541 million years ago. From then to today, there are three eras: Paleozoic, Mesozoic and Cenozoic. No longer content to refer to all geologic time before the Paleozoic era as "Pre-Cambrian," geologists now speak of eons, with time from the "Cambrian Explosion" of life 541 million years ago to the present as the Phanerozoic (visible life) Eon. Instead of just a "Precambrian Supereon," there are now the Proterozoic, Archaean and Hadaen Eons that precede the Phanerozoic, each with its own eras and further subdivisions. Within the Phanerozoic and its three eras are periods (and occasionally ages and epochs). The earliest period of the Paleozoic era is the Cambrian, lasting from 541 million years ago (mya) until 485 mya, when the Ordovician period began. At 444 mya, the Ordovician gave way to the Silurian, which lasted until 419 mya, when the Devonian period began. At 359 mya, the Carboniferous period began, when much of the rock making up the Cumberland Plateau was created. The Carboniferous Period is divided into an early sub-period called the Mississippian and a later sub-period called the Pennsylvanian. This distinction is critical, as the sandstone caprock of the plateau was created during the Pennsylvanian sub-period (from 328 mya to 299 mya), while the softer limestone strata developed during the Mississippian (359 mya to 328 mya). The last period of the Paleozoic era is the Permian, when the supercontinent of Pangaea was created and the Appalachian Mountains reached their peak. A mass extinction at the end of the Permian period, 251 mya, began the Mesozoic era, with its Triassic, Jurassic and Cretaceous periods. After another mass extinction 66 mya, the Cenozoic era began, with its Paleogene, Neogene, Pleistocene and Holocene periods up to today.[30]

By the middle of the nineteenth century, geologists had become familiar with many of these terms and applied them to local studies and surveys. Much of the geological field was driven especially by the intensive search for minerals necessary to fuel the Industrial Revolution. In fact, the use of the term "Pennsylvanian" to refer to the later Carboniferous sub-period was a direct reflection of the importance of coal in the development of geological time scale nomenclature. Scientists in Tennessee were quick to highlight the value of geology in identifying the state's natural resources, including the coal and iron found along the Cumberland Plateau.

Gerard Troost, Tennessee's first state geologist, and his successor, James Safford, published numerous tracts and surveys of the state's mineral resources and rock formations during the mid- to late nineteenth century. Troost was especially interested in the crinoids found in the limestone beds of Middle Tennessee, while Safford focused on the presence of mineral resources.[31] Safford published a geologic map of the state in 1855 that emphasized iron, coal and other natural resources found in "the bosom" of the state.[32] His 1869 book on Tennessee geology included detailed references to rock strata thousands of feet deep, emergence of specific rock formations, folding and faulting of rock and the powers of erosion to carve the landscape. The accompanying map with the 1869 book revealed, among other things, the relationship between soil quality and geologic origin and the effect of folding and faulting on the creation of the mountains of Tennessee. What Safford did not know, however, was the *cause* of the "folding, Dislocation and denudation of Strata in East Tennessee." He could only describe these deformations as "due to great disturbance, and need elucidation."[33] It would take nearly a century for geologists to identify that mysterious force emerging from the east: the colliding of North American and African plates during the formation of the supercontinent Pangaea.

Explorers imagined that the continents had somehow fit together like puzzle pieces as long ago as the sixteenth century. Yet it was not until Alfred Wegener published his theory of continental drift in 1927 that geologists first seriously debated something like plate tectonics.[34] Arguments continued for another thirty years until oceanographers discovered the Mid-Atlantic Rift, a key component of plate tectonic theory. With modern mapping of seismic activity along fault lines around the world and new theories of convection currents from the mantle to explain shifting plates in the lithosphere, scientists finally came to embrace plate tectonic theory. Since that time, much of the mystery behind that "great disturbance" from Tennessee's east has been resolved.

Don Byerly, professor emeritus of geology at the University of Tennessee, recently wrote *The Last Billion Years: A Geologic History of Tennessee* to convey to the general public the latest scholarship on the formation of Tennessee's landscape.[35] As the book title suggests, the origins of Tennessee's landforms go back a billion years—or more like 1.1 billion years—to the formation of a supercontinent called Rodinia. As the mini-plates collided to form Rodinia, a mountain range called the Grenville Mountains developed. Around 600 million years or so ago, Rodinia broke apart, and an ocean formed between proto–North America and the rest of Rodinia. This ocean, named the Iapetus Ocean (Iapetus being the father of Atlas, for whom the Atlantic is named), contained within it several "terranes" or volcanic island chains that continued to meld together and shift places. Two times in the following 300 million years, these terranes rammed into North America and created new mountain ranges: the Taconic orogeny in the Ordovician period and the Acadian orogeny in the Devonian. As each mountain building episode or orogeny ended, erosion started to wear down the peaks. But when fully weathered, the fault lines still existed and so became the sites of future folds and mountains. Much like a piece of foil, when wrinkled once, it will usually fold subsequent times along the same wrinkles.

Another factor is important to keep in mind as well: the existence of a shallow, inland or "epicontinental" sea. Also, as plates shift around, they sometimes lift up or drop. At some point during the Ordivician period, a dome formed over current Nashville and the Ozarks, with the "Pascola Arch" roughly connecting the two.[36] A similar dome near Cincinnati stretched down to the Nashville Dome and formed the Cincinnati Arch.[37] Between the Cincinnati Arch to the west and the Taconic and, later, the Acadian Mountains to the east was the inland sea known generally as the Appalachian Basin. At roughly 350 million years ago, during what geologists call the Mississippian Age, a great variety of sea-based life forms thrived in the Appalachian Basin. Toward the end of the Mississippian Age and the beginning of the Pennsylvanian Age 300 million years ago, life began to appear along the swampy lands at the edge of the Appalachian Basin. As each of these life forms died, their remains collected along the sea and swamp floor and fossilized. Meanwhile, the inland sea continually transgressed and regressed, carrying sediment on top of the fossils and compressing them into a kind of organic rock material.[38] What happened next is essential for understanding the geologic makeup of the Cumberland Plateau.

Beginning around 251 million years ago, the North American and African plates collided and formed the famous supercontinent Pangaea. Near and along the existing fault lines from the Grenville, Taconic and Acadian orogenies, the great Allegheny orogeny created a much larger series of faults and a gigantic mountain range through the heart of Pangaea.[39] This was when the Appalachian Mountain chain reached elevations matching the Himalayas today. But even as the peaks pushed up to the sky, erosion carried sediment off to the west. When the sediment combined with the earliest fossilized remains, it became a black radioactive rock known as Chattanooga shale.[40] When the sediment combined with more substantial organic material from the inland sea, it formed limestone, a very soluble rock. Where it combined with swamp-like reefs along the distant sandy shores, it compressed the material into peat and then coal. And where there was no organic material, the sediment formed layer after layer of erosion-resistant sandstone. The erosion of sediment thus produced a horizontal series of layers visible all along the Cumberland Plateau.

This process of deposition and erosion was not a simple one, however. As plates drifted over the equator and toward the poles, glaciers formed and melted, making the inland sea advance and recede. Each sequence of sea transgression and regression resulted in the deposition of sediment and the eroding and transporting of sediment.[41] Since this occurred very slowly over a long time, the sediment could harden into layers before a different depositional material piled on top of it. The result was a series of interlocked tongues, where sandstone could appear atop shale, atop more sandstone,

Wind erosion creates a boulder garden on Black Mountain in Cumberland County, just north of Grassy Cove.

then coal, then more sandstone (of a different formation) and then limestone. Since different rocks erode at different rates, the landscape reveals distinctive patterns. Sandstone typically forms a caprock and will not erode until most of the layers underneath it have disappeared, at which point it will break into large boulders found in many of the gorges.

To summarize, then, three important geologic forces created the Cumberland Plateau. First was the deposition of different layers of sediment in the Appalachian Basin. Some of these layers included organic material and eroded easily, and others included mostly quartzite sandstone from both the Allegheny orogeny to the east and the Cincinnati Arch to the west. The second force was the tectonic pressure that uplifted the plateau. Because the plateau was far enough to the west, it did not experience the degree of folding and faulting as did the mountains of the Ridge and Valley Province. The three exceptions—the Cumberland Block, Cumberland Mountains and the Sequatchie Valley—resulted from tectonic pressure and folding. The rest simply rose vertically. There have likely been secondary uplifts as well, though geologists are not as certain what caused them. The third great force is erosion, as rivers and air cut away at the rock at different rates. Rivers on the western edge of the plateau followed a "dendritic" or tree-like pattern, with branches cutting into the caprock and creating channels and waterfalls as they made their way down to the Cumberland, Elk and Duck Rivers in Middle Tennessee.[42] Unlike with the sharp escarpment on the eastern plateau, rivers on the west were able to cut more deeply into the plateau, breaking it into pieces. Some solitary plateau pieces called monadnocks remain—like Short Mountain in Cannon County—as evidence of a much wider plateau at one point.[43]

The geologic formation of the Cumberland Plateau explains the origin of resources buried deep "in the bosom" of the earth as well. Coal, as already discussed, resulted from the compression of swampy plants along the edge of the former Appalachian Basin. Pressure from new layers of sedimentation squeezed the gas and liquid from the carbon-heavy layer and formed bituminous coal. Two other major mineral resources—saltpeter and iron—were also produced from geologic forces, though sometimes indirectly. Hematite, an important mineral used to produce iron, appeared in thin beds along Walden Ridge.[44] Because of its proximity to coal and limestone, the hematite beds in Roane, Rhea and Hamilton Counties were important components in the coking and steel-making process. The hematite beds were produced during the Silurian period (444 mya to 416 mya) where the Valley and Ridge meets the plateau. Saltpeter, or potassium nitrate, is created by bat guano in caves along the western edge of the plateau. Used as a basic material for gunpowder, saltpeter was mined and produced in dozens of caves that proliferated in the limestone-rich Mississippian karst of the Highland Rim.

Upon this geologic foundation is the basis for life along the Cumberland Plateau. Sometimes previous life forms are literally caked into the landscape, as in limestone and coal. Later creatures would make their lives either within those organic landscapes or by excavating rock formed by its decayed remains. Plants and, later, animals that make their living on the elevated caprock or within the limestone crevices would replace sea and shoreline creatures of the Mississippian and Pennsylvanian ages. In more recent times, a mixed mesophytic forest emerged, with different tree species occupying different altitudes and soils.[45] Pines mostly on the plateau rim and a diverse array of hardwood trees in the gorges make the Cumberland Plateau the longest forested plateau in the world. Microclimates within the deep gorges produce wildflowers, fungi and rare plants that thrive in this peculiar environment. The wild fauna of the plateau is also diverse, with large and small game thriving in the temperate forest climate. Abundant game naturally attracted humans to the bounties of the plateau.

Humans have traveled across the Cumberland Plateau for over twelve thousand years. Until the arrival of European settlement, however, most peoples have used the plateau as a hunting ground and not for permanent settlement. In fact, the plateau made for a perfect "Long Hunter's" home, with rock houses available to shelter hunters chasing game for months at a time. For hundreds of years, major landmarks along the plateau demarcated boundaries between hunting lands for different native peoples. The Great Stone Door in Savage Gulf, for example, served as a boundary line between the hunting lands of the Cherokee and Chickamauga.[46] Similarly, a standing stone near modern-day Monterey was used for various purposes, including a likely boundary between Cherokee and Shawnee land claims.[47]

We can follow the law of geology—the present as a key to the past—to ask what the geography of the Cumberland Plateau tells us about the Civil War. The landscape carved by deep time, with a nineteenth-century political landscape superimposed on it, makes a few things clear: Cumberland Gap was a deeply important invasion route; Chattanooga was a very difficult, but very important, city to defend; and the coves and hollows along the western Cumberland Plateau made for a perfect breeding ground for guerrilla war. Fortunately, we can rely on more than just a geologic record to tell us what happened during the Civil War on the Cumberland Plateau. People who traded, fought, settled, preached and traveled along the plateau kept rich records of their experiences. Whether in cave graffiti, oral tradition, personal recollections or documents produced by civilian and military government bureaucracies, a record exists for us to examine the Civil War along Tennessee's Cumberland Plateau.

So how, then, did the landscape, sculpted over hundreds of millions of years, affect the events of the nineteenth century and the Civil War? It is tempting to declare that topography and geography "determined" the behavior of people during the Civil War era. After all, as subsequent chapters will discuss in greater detail, most of the Confederate sympathizers tended to live in the western and southern portions of the plateau and in the lower elevations where the soil was more fertile and farmers could afford slaves to produce commercial crops. The northern and eastern parts of the plateau were, by contrast, more isolated; farmers were less likely to own slaves, and the people were more likely to support the Union. This determinist approach taken too far would be a mistake, however. What matters most are the human relationships and networks that developed within the geographic setting of the Cumberland Plateau. And people belonged to multiple social networks at once, with many of them overlapping in complex and troubling ways.[48] Whether based in relationships of kin, church, neighborhood, partisan politics or commerce, social networks could lead otherwise close family members living in the same place to pursue very different courses during the war. Geography went a long way toward shaping many of these networks, and geology helps us understand the physical topographic setting that encouraged them. But ideas traveled far and wide in the nineteenth century. Human agency—individual decisions made by ordinary people—and human-produced social networks often went contrary to the fault lines and dendritic drainage patterns engraved into the earth.[49]

What's more, the way we think about geography has more to do with arbitrary imagined boundaries placed on the land than it does the actual landforms created by nature. In a war where state politics did so much to define loyalties, the line between, say, Tennessee and Kentucky was of critical importance. But that state line followed a latitude line (and a poorly surveyed one at that) rather than a natural barrier like a river or mountain. At the same time, the forces of geology created important landscape markers that occasionally coincided with these man-made boundaries. Such was the case with Cumberland Gap, a boundary of three states and the best natural pathway from east to west and from north to south. The topography of the plateau encouraged trade through some passages—down the Sequatchie

Honey Creek Gorge in Big South Fork National River and Recreation Area.

or the Wolf River or through a gap in the Crab Orchard Mountains, for example—and limited trade in other directions. Meanwhile, the geology of cove and hollow formation encouraged some kinship networks to rely almost entirely on one another for survival.[50] This was especially true for the Beaty family in the East Fork of the Obey River.

Social networks helped to mediate the news of the outside world. Information about troop movements and political ideas passed into the Cumberland Plateau along networks—circuit-riding ministers to local preachers; merchants to commercial farmers and stock raisers; hired laborers to other hired laborers; uncles to nephews and grandmothers to granddaughters; masters to slaves to other slaves and often back to masters again in the form of rumor; county clerks to politicians in Nashville and to political precinct captains and so on. Social networks determined whom one could trust and whom one should avoid.[51] Some of these networks incorporated neighbors within a small geographic space, while others stretched like tentacles down river valleys, turnpikes and railroads to faraway towns. Geography did much to influence the formation of social relationships in the nineteenth-century Cumberland Plateau. But there were many exceptions, too, including individuals who rebelled against their families, or who ran from the law or who avoided unfavorable commercial ties.

The next chapter discusses the permanent settlement of European descendants on the Cumberland Plateau. Most of the people who made a living on the plateau did so on the bounty of the earth—as farmers, miners, blacksmiths and keepers of the house. With some exceptions, the natural landscape dictated where people could settle and what fortune they could expect to obtain living on the land. Also with some exceptions, the natural landscape would influence what kinds of communities developed among the people of the Cumberland Plateau and how they would respond to the crisis of Civil War.

SETTLEMENT AND SOCIETY ON THE CUMBERLAND PLATEAU

P leasant Gatewood was a well-known livestock trader around Pall Mall in Fentress County. Small farmers throughout the neighborhood sold their surplus cattle and mules to Gatewood, hoping to get store goods on cash or credit to keep them through the winter. When farmers came to Gatewood's store, they also heard news about the outside world—hog prices, colorful politicians, bank failures, new canals and railroads and all kinds of other information from places far removed from the Wolf River Valley. On Court Days, banner trading days, farmers passed this information around to one another, along with new rumors and news from around the neighborhood. Gatewood was quite well traveled by the standards of the 1840s and 1850s. Every year, he drove his cattle over to Burrville in Morgan County and then to Kingston and Knoxville. From there, he'd take them the long route up the Great Valley to Baltimore, Maryland, where he'd trade his livestock for Tarskein wagons and all kinds of goods that he knew the folks back in the Wolf River Valley would want. In this way, Pleasant Gatewood served as a conduit for a network of farmers from the Pall Mall neighborhood.[1]

The American Civil War on the Cumberland Plateau was a communal war, with loyalties cutting through neighborhoods, churches and families. The patterns of loyalty reflected divisions in Cumberland Plateau society that were largely hidden until the outbreak of war but were nevertheless rooted in the earliest days of white settlement in the region. Churches belonging to the same denomination often split over sectional questions and the Civil War; even within regional conferences, like the Holston of the Methodist

Church, divisions proved to be violent and permanent.[2] Within the same families, the youngest and oldest siblings might find their close associates pulling them in opposite directions. A bird's-eye view of Cumberland Plateau neighborhoods would not tell the story of neighborhood loyalties because people established social connections through patterns of trade, worship, marriage and migration. Stock traders like Pleasant Gatewood undoubtedly carried great influence among those he knew, but that might not include his kinfolk or his closest neighbors. To understand how these patterns of loyalty developed and how social networks among people of the Cumberland Plateau developed, we must consider the process through which European descendants first settled the land.[3]

As in much of the early trans-Appalachian west, white settlers came from Pennsylvania, Maryland, Virginia or the Carolinas and followed the valleys, turnpikes and mountain gaps into the west. Peoples of various economic classes, from planter sons to recently freed indentured servants, navigated their way through the complex landscape of the Blue Ridge, the Great Valley and the Appalachian Plateau beyond. From Pennsylvania came settlers who encountered southwest-facing mountains past the Susquehanna River. Beginning in the earliest days of the eighteenth century, European settlers pouring into William Penn's colony had sought open and fertile lands to the west. First English Quakers, then Palatine Germans and finally Ulster Scots arrived at the port of Philadelphia and purchased lands from the colony's proprietor, William Penn. A policy of religious tolerance and relative peace with the native population made Pennsylvania a particularly inviting destination for eighteenth-century immigrants escaping the religious wars, enclosure policies and famine in the Old World. The reality of large-scale white settlement brought increasing conflict, however, between whites and French-allied Indians; Scots-Irish and Germans; frontier settlers and the Quaker-dominated legislature; land speculators and squatters; and, eventually, France and Great Britain. For settlers reaching the mountains of central Pennsylvania and western Maryland, the safest and most secure option for continued migration lay to the southwest down the Great Wagon Road and not due west into what was called the Ohio Country.[4] It would not be until the 1780s, after the Revolution and its associated Indian wars, that westward migrants would find more direct westerly traffic more inviting.

Others began in Virginia and picked up the emigrant train in the Shenandoah or Holston Valley. With nutrient-depleted tobacco soils of the Tidewater and Piedmont garnering fewer profits for sons of Virginia planters, many of them sought out new country in the lands surveyed and explored by

Peter Jefferson (Thomas's father), Dr. Thomas Walker, Richard Henderson and Daniel Boone.[5] Surpassing the prodigal planters in number were poorer men and women recently released from the bonds of indentured servitude. These would-be yeomen hoped to gain landownership—a measure of true freedom as it was understood in the eighteenth century—and only in the west could that elusive dream possibly come true. Traveling with these wagon trains were various enslaved Virginians, most of them tasked with the responsibility to clear out forests for new plantations in Kentucky.[6]

Then there were the North and South Carolinians, who, like the Virginians, included a mix of planter pedigree and poor indentures. The Carolina Road had once beckoned many Pennsylvanians—Scots-Irish and German—to move to the Yadkin Valley of North Carolina and the Uplands of South Carolina. But by the 1770s and 1780s, many of these settlers set out again into the western lands beyond the Proclamation Line of 1763, which the British king had marked as the westernmost boundary of legal white settlement. It was primarily this third Carolina-based group that would settle the Cumberland Plateau region, but the Pennsylvanians and Virginians would add significant numbers to the mix.

On the way into the west, settlers first encountered the great Cumberland Escarpment, a seemingly impassable barrier. There were numerous gaps in the Blue Ridge to get into the Great Valley, but to pass beyond the valley proved a far greater challenge. Not only were the Allegheny and Cumberland Plateaus standing in the way, but also other equally formidable barriers lay just beyond. Only Cumberland Gap, and its parallel passage through Pine Mountain at the Narrows, offered a way through to the fertile bluegrass lands of Kentucky. Though the Cherokee and Shawnee had long known of the Cumberland Gap's importance as a thoroughfare to the hunting grounds of Kentucky, it was the hundreds of thousands of white settlers who followed Daniel Boone's Wilderness Road through the gap that made it so important in both regional and national history.[7] From 1780 until 1810, as many as 300,000 settlers made their way through Cumberland Gap and into Kentucky.

Nearly all of these settlers passed through Cumberland Gap with little or no intention of remaining in the vicinity of the gap. However, some business-minded settlers saw the opportunity to sell produce and supplies to these westward migrants. Between Cumberland Mountain and Powell Mountain to the southeast lay the Powell River, which cut a fertile valley running southwesterly from Big Stone Gap, Virginia, past Cumberland Gap to Caryville in Campbell County. Several "stations" or "stands" appeared

Wolf River Valley

Sgt. York in World War I

The Wolf River Valley is connected to the very origins of Tennessee history. Indians hunted this valley, fished in the river and blazed trails centuries before Europeans explored the region. Daniel Boone and his brother, Squire, spent the winter of 1769 in a cave in Pall Mall and named a number of places in the Upper Cumberland. Scores of longhunters followed the Boones, as did Coonrod Pile (buried here), a German ancestor of Alvin C. York and the first permanent settler of Pall Mall around the time Tennessee became a state.

Mark Twain

One of Coonrod's neighbors and contemporaries was John Marshall Clemens, credited with naming the area "Pall Mall" after an elite London, England, neighborhood. Clemens held numerous positions in early Fentress County and was the father of Sam, better known as "Mark Twain," who wrote about the area calling it the "Knobs of Obedstown" in his book *The Gilded Age*.

Civil War

The Civil War divided the region, and families literally did fight and kill each other. Tinker Dave Beaty and Confederate guerrilla Champ Ferguson used the war to settle personal scores. Governor Isham Harris established a training camp in Pall Mall near Rotten Fork. Camp McGinnis was home to more than 10,000 soldiers, the most people this valley has ever seen at once.

On Sept. 29, 1861, the first military action of the war in Tennessee took place at Travisville, five miles north of here. 100 Soldiers from Camp McGinnis led a raid into Kentucky in one of the first invasions of the north by Confederate troops. They caught Federal troops unaware, stealing hundreds of pounds of gunpowder, and headed back to Tennessee. Thinking they had outrun the enemy, they made camp around the Travisville Methodist Church along Caney Creek. Soon Federal troops descended on them. Four Confederates were killed in this clash while the remaining troops retreated into the surrounding hills.

"Uncle Billy" Hull, father of Secretary of State and Father of the United Nations Cordell Hull, was left for dead after being shot in the face. He lived to track and kill the would-be assassins.

Coonrod Pile's grandson, Rod, was hauled out of his home, shot 13 times and left in the road to die by six of Champ Ferguson's men. His mother, Rebecca, recognized his assailants and vowed revenge. Five of the six were pursued and killed by Rod's brothers long after the war ended.

A historic sign describes several layers of history converging in the Wolf River Valley in Pall Mall, Tennessee.

in the Powell Valley as early as 1783, offering merchandise to travelers through the region. Following Richard Henderson's large land purchase in the area, the Gibson, Chisum, Graham, Martin, Yoakum and many other families established market-oriented farms and stations in the valley.[8] Serving the legions of migrants passing through nearby Cumberland Gap or southwesterly into Tennessee, the Powell Valley farms and stations were among the first permanent white settlements along the Cumberland Plateau.

Not all Wilderness Road travelers turned toward Cumberland Gap. Many North Carolinians established semi-independent communities along the Watauga River as early as the late 1760s, including Sycamore Shoals. For the next twenty-five years, the legal status of the western lands changed at a dizzying pace, sometimes due to Indian wars and treaties and other times because of Revolutionary and constitutional events. Until the 1830s, settlement in what came to be the states of Kentucky and Tennessee was fraught with legal uncertainty. Widespread violation of the Proclamation Line of 1763, which forbade English settlement beyond the crest of the Appalachian Mountains, created a veritable zone of anarchy in the Old Southwest. In an early "dangerous example" of self-government, settlers near Sycamore Shoals established the Watauga Association in 1771 after North Carolina continually refused to protect these proclamation violators against the Cherokee. North Carolina had long claimed ownership of the lands west to the Mississippi River and placed the trans-Appalachian region under the jurisdiction of "Washington County." This included mostly the Watauga Association lands but later came to include settlements south and west to the junction of the Tennessee and Clinch Rivers.[9]

After the Revolution, this troublesome "Washington County" section attempted to separate from North Carolina and form the fourteenth state of Franklin. The Franklinites seceded from North Carolina for much the same reason that the Watauga settlement was laid out: to secure landholdings without paying taxes to the North Carolina government and to provide for militia defense against Indians. A brief and somewhat comical "war" between Franklin and anti-Franklin forces resulted in the new state's disappearance by 1787. The episode would become one of many that highlighted the weakness of the Articles of Confederation and the need for a stronger federal Constitution.[10]

At the same time, a series of negotiations between North Carolina and Virginia land speculators and Cherokee leaders led to the "purchase" of massive tracts of land in the "Transylvania" country. Some of that land, including much of Kentucky, was not the Cherokee's to give away (it being primarily the hunting lands of the rival Shawnee). More troublesome to many Cherokee, however, was the forfeiture of lands along the Little Tennessee River. This series of treaties, beginning with the 1776 Treaty of the Holston, forced the removal of Cherokee families from the Upper Tennessee River Valley. Many Cherokee rejected these treaties, moved to the southwest, reorganized as the Chickamauga and vowed to reclaim the lands they felt had been stolen. Warfare between white settlers and Chickamauga, complicated by dubious alliances with Spain, continued for the next twenty-five years. Forts guarded white settlement in the southern sections of the newly acquired lands. Some of them developed into sizable and prosperous towns, while others disappeared without a trace. By 1795, however, ruthless attacks from John Sevier and others forced the Cherokee's permanent evacuation of much of the Upper Tennessee Valley.[11] Of all the territory north of the Tennessee River Gorge and the southern Unaka Mountains, only the sparsely settled Cumberland Plateau remained under nominal Cherokee control.

From 1779 on, many North Carolinians bypassed Washington County in favor of the Cumberland River Valley two hundred miles to the west. Here the soil was richer even than the bottomlands of the Tennessee River. News of the so-called Cumberland settlements around the future city of Nashville quickly reached Virginia and North Carolina, including those with means to travel and establish farms and even plantations. When the Revolutionary War ended in 1783, the North Carolina government encouraged Revolutionary War veterans to stake claims to land in the Cumberland settlements, much as Virginia did in Kentucky and southern Ohio.[12]

With ratification of the new Constitution in 1788, these contested and legally tenuous western lands were ceded to the federal government. The region, now called the Territory South and West of the Ohio River, or Southwest Territory, contained a string of settlements along the Nolichucky, Watauga, Powell, Holston, French Broad and Clinch Rivers, as well as a series of communities along the lower bend of the Cumberland River. Its governor, William Blount, established his headquarters at the new city of Knoxville, where the Holston and French Broad Rivers meet. By 1795, the Southwest Territory included two well-established settlement areas: the Washington District to the east centered on Knoxville and stretching north and east to North Carolina and the western Cumberland River basin centered on the new city of Nashville and renamed the (inadvertently misspelled) "Mero District" in honor of Spanish Louisiana governor Miro in hopes of securing Spanish protection in the ongoing wars against Indians. In between the Washington and Mero Districts was the Cumberland Plateau, still mostly unsettled by whites and nominally controlled by Cherokee and Chickamauga eager to stem the tide of white encroachment.[13]

By the next year, the populations of both districts necessitated the creation of a new state, Tennessee, with its capital at Knoxville. A constitutional convention met at Knoxville and petitioned for admission to the Union as the sixteenth state of Tennessee. Heady optimism about western settlement in lands now largely cleared of Indians characterized the early development of the state. As thousands of migrants poured into the Upper Tennessee Valley and sought farms and homesteads in the Cumberland River Basin to the west, the new state government quickly discovered a pressing need for improved transportation over the plateau.

Here, then, was the moment when sizable settlement of the Cumberland Plateau began, and it was driven mostly by migrants passing over the tableland with no intentions of settling permanently. It was always possible to bypass the plateau, just as two early Cumberland settlement leaders had done. James Robertson had set out in 1780, going through Cumberland Gap into Kentucky and then via a series of small river journeys and portages to reach the bend of the Cumberland from the north. John Donelson, on the other hand, took the Tennessee River the entire way, past the hostile Chickamauga towns and through the sucks and shoals of the lower bend before reaching the Ohio River, turning upstream and then embarking up the Cumberland to his destination. But for the majority of migrants, neither of these dangerous, costly and circuitous paths was very appealing. Successive governmental bodies—the North Carolina legislature, the federal Southwest Territory government and the Tennessee legislature—commissioned the surveying and construction of a turnpike to cross the plateau and link the two settlement areas directly. As it turned out, several turnpikes would be built, with each one rivaling the other for business.[14]

The first path began just northeast of Knoxville at the foot of Clinch Mountain, near the modern community of Blaine. Roughly following the current Emory Road and Tennessee State Route 62, the route, known by many as the Avery Trace, punched through the Cumberland Escarpment at Winters Gap (now Oliver Springs) and traversed the southern part of what became Morgan County. Beyond that, the Avery Trace reached the Standing Stone (at modern Monterey) and continued west-northwesterly toward the Cumberland River at Fort Blount, just east of Carthage. From there, the road continued through Castallian Springs and then reached Nashville from the north side of the river.[15]

The so-called Avery Trace roughly followed an old Cherokee path known as Tallonteeskee's Trail, which itself traced old buffalo trails and hunting paths centuries old. The trace was poorly constructed, with the roadbed collapsing regularly. And it was far too narrow for large-scale migration or trade.

By 1801, the Tennessee legislature had commissioned the construction of a far more reliable and permanent turnpike known as the Walton Road. Officially called the Cumberland Turnpike, the Walton Road did more to open travel across the plateau and settlement on it than any other singular event. The Walton Road began just to the southwest of Kingston. Roughly following the current U.S. 70 and U.S. 70N, the Walton Road climbed the Cumberland Escarpment at Kimbrough Gap (just west of modern-day Rockwood) past the Ozone Falls and Crab Orchard Mountains to the Standing Stone. From that point on, it largely tracked the older Avery Trace, though with significant construction improvements. By 1805, white settlement over the plateau had become so robust that the Cherokee were persuaded to cede the land to Tennessee in the Third Treaty of Tellico.[16]

Just as was the case near Cumberland Gap, the Walton Road beckoned commercial-oriented farmers to establish stands, stations and taverns to

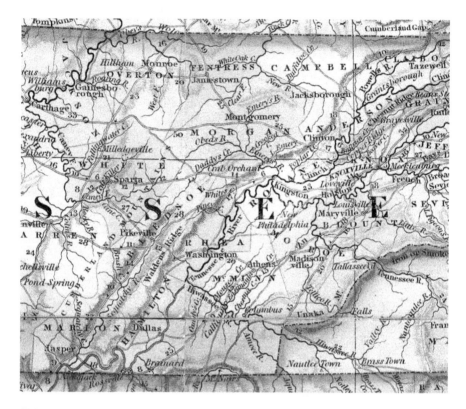

This 1834 map of Tennessee shows turnpikes crossing the Cumberland Plateau. *Courtesy of Tennessee Digital Map Library, USGenWeb Archives.*

serve westward migrants. Unlike the Powell Valley settlements, however, the Walton Road stands appeared on top of the Cumberland Plateau and so were among the first to attempt to farm the notoriously thin and rocky soil. A popular spot was the Sidnor Stand near Crab Orchard Mountain, a particularly dangerous spot for travelers. For those attempting to cross the Obed River, Graham's Stand offered respite for the weary traveler. When the Walton Road was completed, a new and improved hostel, known as Johnson's Stand, was built across the river from Graham's Stand.[17]

Over the course of the next fifty years, other turnpikes would be constructed across the plateau. Some, like the Gordon Turnpike and Burke Road, roughly paralleled the Walton Road and competed for business with the main "Stage Road." Others, like the Kentucky Stock Road and the Pile Turnpike, passed southward from Fentress County and into the central plateau area. As settlement continued down the Tennessee River, new turnpikes would connect the towns cleared of

Cherokee in the 1830s with the prosperous farms of the Nashville basin. The Washington and Jefferson Turnpike, beginning at Washington's Ferry in Rhea County, bisected the Sequatchie Valley at Pikeville and continued in a northwestern fashion toward Sparta and Middle Tennessee. The Anderson Turnpike, which would play an important role in the battles around Chattanooga, was built by Josiah Anderson and passed over Signal Mountain into the lower Sequatchie settlements. And the Georgia Road would be developed between Hale's Bar near the Tennessee River and Murfreesboro, ascending Monteagle Mountain in the process. Smaller turnpikes were authorized by the legislature extending into Powell's Valley and Sequatchie Valley.[18]

Enterprising commercial farmers hoped that steamboat traffic along the Tennessee River, beginning in the 1820s, would provide riches for valley cities and plateau market stands. A robust trade between Chattanooga, Kingston and Knoxville attracted many hog raisers and corn farmers. But as the Tennessee River meandered its way west of Chattanooga and into a maze of sucks and shoals, its commercial value dimmed for upriver traders. For most of the year, the Tennessee River was simply not navigable past Chattanooga. Alas, the economic limits of East Tennessee quickly revealed themselves, as fertile soil was limited to the lowest bottomland, and the great Tennessee River proved to be mostly a dead end.

Still, the limited Tennessee River trade attracted commercial farmers from the Sequatchie Valley, where farmers supplied basic foodstuffs for the growing cotton plantations in Alabama. Just west of the plateau in Franklin County were some of the first cotton plantations to be established west of Georgia. The trade and political networks between commercial Sequatchie farmers and Franklin County and Alabama cotton planters would influence loyalty patterns in the Civil War.[19]

Even more influential than the steamboat was the development of several railroads along the periphery of the plateau in the 1850s. Prior to the Civil War, only one railroad actually passed over the plateau. The Nashville and Chattanooga Railroad passed through the Cowan Tunnel and over the southwestern edge of the plateau on its voyage from Nashville to Stevenson, Alabama.[20] A branch line ascended Sewanee Mountain and ran through Tracy City and its coalfields. The East Tennessee and Georgia, East Tennessee and Virginia and Memphis and Charleston Railroads did not actually run across the Cumberland Plateau. But their influences on commercial activities on the plateau were unmistakable, especially on the burgeoning city of Chattanooga.[21]

Boats required special winches to make their way through the sucks and shoals of the Tennessee River Gorge.

For the vast majority of Cumberland Plateau settlers, these developing transportation networks had an indirect effect on daily life. In fact, most people living on the plateau either did not own land or owned tiny plots of land from which they made little or no money from commercial farming. As was true in much of the Old Southwest, eastern speculators purchased most of the Cumberland Plateau land and then reparceled the mostly unsurveyed land to renters and squatters. The practice of encouraging large-scale land grants actually increased in the early nineteenth century, with five-thousand-acre land grants made available to wealthy speculators in 1830. Thomas Eastland, John McCormick, Stephen Haight and John G. Smith collectively owned most of the land in the central part of the plateau in the 1830s.[22]

The result was a population of well-connected merchants in plateau towns like Sparta, Pikeville, Jamestown and Jasper but a majority scattered on very small farm parcels with little to no property at all. According to the 1860 manuscript census, 47 percent of all Cumberland Plateau household heads did not own any real estate.[23] They typically reported their occupations to the census taker as "farm laborer" or "day laborer," with a very small handful reporting skilled trades like blacksmithing or milling. While nearly half the population rented its land, more than 90 percent at least owned some amount of personal property. This could include farm tools, furniture, livestock or other personal possessions. These semi-subsistence farmers toiled on rocky soil and raised most of their foodstuffs with family labor, trading only occasionally with outside markets for peripheral goods. For outside goods, they relied on people like Pleasant Gatewood.

Place names reflected the difficult circumstances of survival for ordinary settlers on the plateau. Names like "No Business Creek," "Brimstone Creek" and various rock formations given devilish monikers like Devil's Racetrack, Devil's Breakfast Table and Devilstep Hollow signified the unforgiving landscape upon which people eked out a living. Naming practices for children also reflected interesting elements. Children were often named either for other kinfolk or given unusual and creative names meant to distinguish individual family members in communities where so many people shared the same surname. Just outside Jamestown, for example, three men named Nathaniel Mullinix, two named A.J. Mullinix and two named Elizabeth Mullinix lived in households near one another; one can infer that the children, grandchildren, nephews and nieces were named for their Mullinix elders. Some children were named for important regional or international figures, like Henry Clay Rains or Bounepartus Huddleston, and some for places, like Tennessee Smith and America Owens. And then there were names that were unusual, even for their time, like Zibber Price, Tranquilla McGee, Zorababel Stephens and the three brothers Winter, White and Snow Frost. Naming practices reflected the respect accorded to kinfolk while conferring individuality on members within extended kinship networks.[24]

There are some important variations in household wealth between counties. In Morgan County, where large numbers of German immigrants settled in the 1840s and generally did not become large-scale commercial farmers, only 30 percent of households rented their land. In Marion County, by contrast, the largely Irish railroad workers and hardscrabble renters on Walden Ridge were less likely to own their own land, with as much as 60

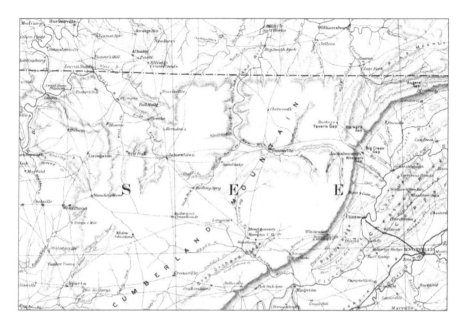

Sparse settlement on the Cumberland Plateau, with turnpikes connecting the county seats. *Maps accompanying* OR.

percent reporting zero real estate wealth. However, the renters of Marion County were still likely to own a degree of personal property, with only 5 percent reporting none. By contrast, in extremely rugged Campbell and Van Buren Counties, 17 percent of the households owned neither real nor personal property. There, residents eked out a living by working on neighboring farms, many of which were owned by kin. Relationships of economic dependence would play an important role in building and cementing social networks on the plateau.[25]

Kinship networks proved especially important for community survival and development on the plateau. The manuscript census register for each county reads like a modern-day telephone book, with clusters of households with common surnames living in proximity. In the Cassville section of western White County, the widow Nancy Anderson, fifty-four years of age, lived adjacent to three farms owned by her three sons, R.J., Archie and J.M. Anderson. In the 1830s, Nancy Anderson's husband, Jabaz, passed away, and the court placed Nancy in the custody of her children.[26]

Brothers Isaac and James Hillis were among the earliest settlers along the Rocky River in western Van Buren County. Isaac Sr. was married twice and produced twenty-one children in all, so there were plenty of family members to settle the rolling farmland in the Rocky River Valley. Proud of their ancestral lineage, subsequent generations of Hillises applied the names Isaac and James to sons, nephews and grandchildren of the original settlers. By 1860, five families with the surname of Hillis appear in the census in succession, with the households headed by Oliver, Squire, James, Isaac and Roswell Hillis. More Hillis surnames appear just across the Rocky River in eastern Warren County; county lines mattered little, as kinship networks followed the natural terrain more than they were defined and constrained by artificial lines on a map. Each of the Hillises owned a middling amount of personal property, though only Oliver and Isaac laid claim to real estate wealth in 1860. As is typical of tightknit Cumberland Plateau communities, many of the Hillises are buried in a family cemetery on land donated by Blackstone Oregon Hillis in the decades after the Civil War.[27]

In Sweedens Cove in Marion County, two families populated most of the settlement: the Beenes and Raulstons. There was plenty of intermarrying between the two families over the years, but they kept remarkably separate. In fact, they likely developed something of a rivalry with each other, as

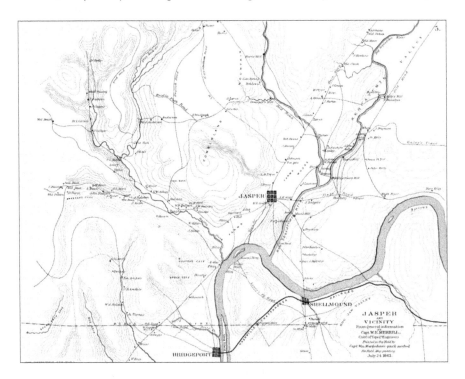

Interlocking families in Sweedens Cove. *Maps accompanying* OR.

the Beenes mostly supported the Confederacy during the Civil War and the Raulstons sided with the Union.[28] Relations may have patched up in later years, as members of both families are buried in the Bean-Roulston Cemetery near South Pittsburg.

Intermarriage among neighboring families was common, with children and grandchildren often named for some of the earliest settlers on the plateau. In the early 1820s, an early settler in Jacksboro named Elisha Adkins married a cousin, Rebecca Adkins, whose mother was Rachel McCoy. By 1860, several families with the surname of Adkins and McCoy continued to live next to one another. A wealthy neighbor of Elisha Adkins, named Caswell Queener, was an uncle of Julia Ann Queener, who married a grandchild of Elisha Adkins—also named Elisha—in the 1880s. Ties of kinship helped bridge class divisions and likely nurtured important political and military loyalties.[29]

Perhaps the most consequential kinship network on the Cumberland Plateau was the Beaty family, who settled along the East Fork of the Obey River in the Boatland section of western Fentress County. George, David and John Beaty all arrived in the valley of the East Fork in the 1810s. George's wife, Lydia Ann Wilson, gave birth to a son named David Crockett Beaty. By 1860, the neighborhood along the East Fork was dotted with households led by men named Beaty, Choate, Crockett, Wright and Franklin.[30] In this case, a close-knit network of kin formed the nucleus of one of the Civil War's most effective Unionist guerrilla forces, with David "Tinker Dave" Beaty commanding his Independent Scouts in a long and deadly running battle with his archrival Champ Ferguson.

Kinship networks also formed around immigrant groups, especially those arriving from Germany and settling in Wartburg in Morgan County. The East Tennessee Land Colonization Company, founded by George Gerding, was designed to encourage German families struggling in the difficult economic times of the 1840s to immigrate to America and settle the tablelands of Morgan County. Gerding named the settlement Wartburg after the castle where Martin Luther sought protection against persecution from the Catholic Church. Hundreds of German immigrants settled on plots of land throughout Morgan County, with most in Wartburg and the Pine Top section in the northern part of the county. Compared to the average Cumberland Plateau farmer, these German settlers lived prosperously. Nearly all of them owned their own land in 1860, with many taking up skilled trades or opening shops. Still, many of the German immigrants were bitterly disappointed in the quality of the land and simply moved on to other areas

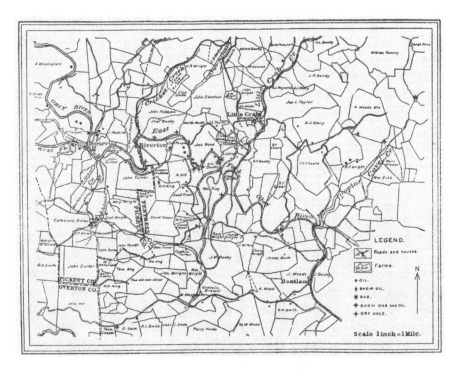

Above: A farm map of the East Fork of the Obey River in Fentress County. This tightly connected valley was Tinker Dave Beaty's stomping ground. *Hougue*, History of Fentress County, Tennessee, *p. 33.*

Right: German and Swiss settlement of Wartburg by the East Tennessee Land Colonization Company.

of the country. One of the few immigrant enclaves in antebellum Tennessee, Morgan County's Germans intermarried frequently with English speakers and generally melded into the larger plateau population.[31]

The Cumberland Plateau contained few sizable urban settlements compared to the Nashville Basin or the Tennessee River Valley. That said, market-oriented towns of regional significance appeared in every plateau county. In each case, kinship networks and clusters proved to be just as important among merchants and craftsmen as they did among the farmers and farm laborers of the country. In Sparta, for example, the Dibrell and Gibbs families stood at the center of law and commerce in White County for decades. Anthony Dibrell and George Gibbs both arrived in Sparta in the early nineteenth century, with Gibbs marrying Dibrell's sister. Anthony Dibrell and his wife, Mildred, named one of their sons George Gibbs Dibrell in honor of the Gibbs ancestors. All of them would be important business partners in antebellum Sparta and beyond, with George Gibbs taking leadership of the Union Bank in Nashville. Anthony Dibrell began his career in banking as well and then became treasurer for the state, a state legislator and receiver of the Sparta land office, a post that kept him in contact with many rural White County residents. George Dibrell likewise began his career in banking and then married Mary Leftwick, the daughter of a Sparta merchant. Until the outbreak of war, George Dibrell served as one of Sparta's wealthiest and most enterprising commercial farmers and merchants. That he would emerge as one of the county's leading military figures was of little surprise, as he had already carved out a place among Sparta's antebellum elite.[32]

The kin and trade networks linked town and country, thus providing even the most isolated farmer access to the news and material goods circulating more broadly. Elite family connections smoothed the way for commercial production and export of cereal crops from fertile valley and cove farms through market towns and beyond. Intermarriage between large landowners and town merchants undoubtedly solidified these commercial agricultural networks. When John Montgomery Crockett Dibrell, brother of George Dibrell and clerk in the Bank of Tennessee branch of Sparta, married Mary Eastland, whose father came from one of the largest landowning families on the Cumberland Plateau, his business ties were significantly enhanced.[33]

Not every plateau farmer participated in trade equally; many rural residents left their immediate neighborhoods so rarely that it appeared the towns and county seats were worlds away. But even those most local-oriented farmers knew of fellow farmers and family members who traveled to town on occasion—to appear in court; to purchase extra supplies; to sell surplus corn, hogs or wheat; to visit with kin—so that news could reach everybody, however slowly. There was always a Pleasant Gatewood around. The Cumberland Plateau may have been one of the most geographically isolated sections of the eastern United States in 1860, but even there, news of the wider world infiltrated every gorge, hollow and ridge-top settlement.

What lines of kinship and commerce reveal more than anything is the mental geography of the people living along the Cumberland Plateau. To the majority of the people who farmed on a semi-subsistence basis, their mental geography included a circumscribed area of farms linked by kinship and labor. Children of one small farmer might work as laborers or domestics for neighboring farmers, many of whom were also kin. The result for most plateau residents was a closely linked world marked both by the physical boundaries imposed by nature and erosion and by cultural boundaries reinforced through generations of mutually dependent labor. In a world where literacy beyond a basic rudimentary level was limited and newspapers rarely circulated among poorer farmers, oral transmission of information and rumor counted as reliable news.[34] And when the source for locally circulated news could be ascribed to a respected elder—regardless of wealth—community members were more likely to accept it as truth.

For market-oriented farmers, merchants, millers and tradesmen, the imagined world of commerce, kin and country spread farther out of the small towns and rural hamlets and incorporated other farmers and merchants from neighboring counties or even states. Newspapers, filled with commercial news, were more influential among commercial farmers than simple oral transmission; the reporting of changing market prices of sorghum, saltpeter, corn and hogs dictated the interpretation of news and events far and wide. Still, the commercial world of even the most sophisticated plateau merchants was mediated by local kinship relations, both to fellow elites and to less fortunate cousins and siblings toiling on nearby farms.[35]

It would be impossible to capture the dynamics of Cumberland Plateau social relations without looking seriously at the institution of slavery. Historians have largely overlooked the incidence and importance of chattel slavery on the Cumberland Plateau, both because the number of slaves was minimal compared to other sections of Tennessee and because so many of the farms operated on a semi-subsistence basis with only family labor at hand. Slavery played a far more defining role in the social, economic and political life of the Cumberland Plateau than the paucity of slaves would suggest. Though historians no longer claim that the Cumberland Plateau—like the rest of Appalachia—was somehow a slave-less egalitarian Eden, few have bothered to study the institution on the plateau in depth.

Table 1

Cumberland Plateau Slave Population by County

County	Population	Slaves	Percentage Enslaved
Anderson	7,068	583	8%
Bledsoe	4,459	689	15%
Campbell	6,712	366	5%
Claiborne	9,643	743	8%
Cumberland	3,460	121	3%
Fentress	5,054	187	4%
Franklin	13,848	3,551	26%
Grundy	3,093	266	9%
Hamilton	13,258	1,419	11%
Marion	6,190	678	11%
Morgan	3,353	120	4%
Overton	12,637	1,087	9%
Putnam	8,558	682	8%
Rhea	4,991	615	12%
Roane	13,583	1,748	13%
Scott	3,519	59	2%
Sequatchie	2,120	201	9%
Van Buren	2,581	239	9%
Warren	11,147	2,320	21%
White	9,381	1,145	12%
Plateau Total	**144,655**	**16,819**	**12%**
Tennessee	**1,109,801**	**275,719**	**25%**

The institution of slavery bore a direct and indirect relationship to social life on the plateau. Slaveholders occupied the most fertile lands and reported a disproportionate share of the region's personal wealth. Though the average slaveholder on the plateau owned fewer than six slaves, the size of slaveholdings varied widely, with the largest slaveholders in each county owning far more than the twenty slaves that qualified them as "planters" in the census (though, tellingly, none of the large slaveholders reported his occupation to the census taker as "planter," choosing instead to refer to himself as "farmer").[36]

In most counties, the largest slaveholders owned far more bondsmen and women than other slaveholders in the county. John Kincaid of Campbell County, for example, owned fifty-four slaves on his farm in the fertile Powell Valley. Of the sixty-two slaveholders in Campbell County, however, only Kincaid and William Sweat owned more than twenty. In fact, the median slaveholder in Campbell County owned three slaves, a number that underscores the disproportionate share of slaveholdings held by just two men. A similar pattern held true in the other counties of the Upper Cumberland, including Cumberland, Morgan and Scott, where slaveholders were few and far between and many neighborhoods were devoid of any slaves. Moreover, while one or two families owned substantial numbers of slaves, most slaveholders in the Upper Cumberland owned fewer than four.

In certain areas, however, several neighboring families owned slaves. In the Pall Mall section of northern Fentress County, several neighboring members of the McGinnis, Huff and Miller families owned slaves on their own farms. Kinship thus tied together patterns of slave ownership, with many slaves likely hired out (formally or informally) among the network of families in Pall Mall. Similarly, in the fertile sinkhole valley of Grassy Cove of Cumberland County, Worthington Greer owned twenty-two slaves, with many of his neighbors, including members of the Kemmer, Ford and Hinch families, owning slaves as well. In the Crown Point area of northern Marion County, the Sheltons, Kelleys and Prigmores each owned slaves in proximity to one another. In the central and southern part of the Cumberland Plateau, slaveholding was more common than it was in the Upper Cumberland. This was especially true in the lower-elevation communities along the Calfkiller River in White County, up and down the Sequatchie Valley, in the Tennessee River bottomlands just east of Walden's Ridge and, especially, in the level plains just west of the southern plateau in Warren and Franklin Counties.

Not all slaves worked in agriculture or as domestics. The Nashville and Chattanooga Railroad, which passed through much of Marion County, employed slave laborers to work along the track, as well as in the coal mines at Tracy City. Operators of resorts like Beersheba Springs in Grundy County typically owned sizable numbers of slaves to cater to guests visiting from the Deep South. Until 1860, the owner and operator of Beersheba Springs was former slave trader John Armfield, whose $200,000 fortune was built on the shipment of thousands of slaves from Virginia to cotton plantations in the Old Southwest.[37] After Armfield retired from the slave-trading business in the 1840s, he purchased the Beersheba Springs Hotel and served many of the cotton planters he had met during his days in the slave trade. Like other springs and resort owners in the mountain South, Armfield solidified social, political and financial connections between the Cumberland Plateau's hospitality industry and its Deep South planter clientele.

Beyond the labor commanded of slaves were the property values embedded in the institution and the status accorded to owners of slaves. The vast majority of Cumberland Plateau residents did not live in households with slaves. But a good percentage of them aspired to become slaveholders and sought the support of the slaveholding elite when faced with poor harvests or other personal travails. Though only 10 percent of plateau households actually owned slaves, slaveholders owned half the region's real estate wealth and 63 percent of the personal wealth. This is hardly surprising, as "prime age" slaves were assessed at $900 each—by far the most expensive form of personal property owned on the Cumberland Plateau or in the South as a whole.

Gendered ideals reflected the multiple social networks of plateau residents. For subsistence farmers, men and women were both expected to contribute manual labor to operate the farmstead. Women headed many plateau households in 1860, with some in charge of extensive families. Lucinda Kenney, a forty-nine-year-old weaver in Hale's Mills in Fentress County, headed a household of seven children. With just $110 in personal property, Kenney depended on the help of her older children to run the house. She might also rely on wealthier neighbors like Dr. Jonathan Hale or Rufus Dowdy, a carpenter with a large family of his own. When the war broke out, Hale and Dowdy would be among the most important Unionists of Fentress County; Dowdy would become a feared Unionist guerrilla and would depend on women in his household and neighboring women like Lucinda Kenney as a supply line for their operations.[38]

Commercially driven farmers and merchants mimicked the paternalist ideal of the plantation lowlands, whose masters and mistresses often doubled as marriageable partners for plateau elites. Rarely did plateau residents adopt the pretensions of Lower South planters by calling themselves "Lady" and "Gentleman" to the census taker. One exception was Thomas Eldridge, a fifty-eight-year-old man of Livingston in Overton County, who referred to himself as a "Gentleman of Leisure," though his middling fortune of $300 in personal property hardly justified the moniker. That said, his close neighbors included the prominent hotelkeeper and future Confederate colonel John M. Hughs and leading merchants of Livingston like W.H. Turner and A.J. Goodbar.[39] Though Thomas Eldridge did not own slaves, cousins of his living nearby did, as did most of his neighbors. In many ways, then, he exemplified the "master of small worlds" so often found among status-conscious small farmers and businessmen.[40] Far removed from the plantation wealth of the Deep South, many small Cumberland Plateau farmers and slaveholders nonetheless imagined themselves to be among the same elite class.[41]

Commercial farmers, millers, merchants and manufacturers traded with slave societies in the Lower South, profited off the slave economy, considered themselves integral parts of a larger southern regional slave-based society and came to the political defense of that slave society whenever its leaders felt threatened. That said, antebellum politics on the Cumberland Plateau rarely centered on the protection of slavery. A vigorous two-party system encouraged plateau voters to participate in the Whig and Democratic Parties and support candidates with competing visions of the role of the government in the economy and with rival patronage networks. Both parties vowed to defend slavery when under attack. Tennessee's two-party system survived the implosion of the national Whig Party in the early 1850s as competing regional loyalties and economic visions surrounding the construction of railroads, banks and public schools occupied much of the state's political attention.[42]

Tennessee's partisan loyalties, which first emerged in the aftermath of President Andrew Jackson's selection of a non-Tennessean—Martin Van Buren—as his successor, continued to hold true across the state and on the plateau. By 1840, partisan loyalties had appeared in strength on the plateau and changed very little over the next twenty years. The Whig William Henry Harrison won Campbell (including future Scott County), Morgan (with part of future Cumberland and Scott Counties), Roane (also including much of future Cumberland County), Bledsoe and Marion Counties, while the Democrat Martin Van Buren took Fentress, Overton, Warren (including future Grundy County) and Franklin Counties. This pattern held true for each subsequent election, with shifts coming mostly because of changing county boundaries—e.g., the redrawing of the Morgan County border made the county more Democratic, with the pro-Whig Scott and Cumberland Counties left behind. Some of the new counties formed in the 1830s and 1840s bore partisan implications at their inception; Van Buren County, created from Warren and White Counties in 1839, immediately cast itself in the Democratic column, as did the county named for Jackson's Democratic champion in Tennessee, Felix Grundy. The county named for the 1852 Whig Party presidential nominee, Winfield Scott, became an instant Whig stronghold.

The Bell-Everett ticket represented the Constitutional Union Party, supported mostly by old-line Whigs.

National elections reflected local party loyalties in the Cumberland Plateau as competing machines energized the entire population in the wake of the 1834 state constitution granting the right to vote to all white men. County courthouses became cliques and centers of local power, with politicians eagerly fighting attempts to dilute their authority through the creation of new counties. Putnam, Cumberland and Sequatchie Counties were created in the 1850s, and they faced vigorous opposition from neighboring county leaders worried about loss of power.[43]

All politics was not local, however, as many prominent plateau politicians and attorneys went on to state and national prominence. John Catron of White County was chosen to serve on the United States Supreme Court and concurred in the famous *Dred Scott* decision in 1857. Peter Turney, a Democrat of Franklin County, was the son of a United States senator and one of the state's most prominent supporters of secession after the election of President Lincoln in 1860. His influence could be felt very strongly in Franklin, Marion, Sequatchie and Grundy Counties in the first half of 1861.

The pattern of partisan division in local and national election continued into the crucial 1860 presidential election. Four candidates ran for president, though only three of them appeared on ballots in Tennessee. Stephen Douglas, nominee of the "Northern" Democratic Party convention, won few votes in Tennessee; Republican Abraham Lincoln received zero votes in the state. The "Southern" Democratic candidate, John C. Breckinridge of Kentucky, won Morgan, Fentress, Overton, Van Buren, Warren, Grundy and Franklin Counties. John Bell, nominated by the Constitutional Union Party and candidate of former Whigs in the Upper South, took Campbell, Scott, Cumberland, White, Bledsoe, Sequatchie and Marion Counties. Once again, the counties of the Cumberland Plateau voted just as they had in every election going back to 1840. Democratic counties stayed in the Democratic column, and Whig Counties continued to vote for the successors to the Whig Party: the American Party, the Opposition and the Constitutional Union Party.

Importantly, voter preference in the 1860 presidential election did not necessarily indicate support or opposition to secession. Many Fentress and Morgan County supporters of Breckinridge followed their state party leader, Andrew Johnson of Greene County, and remained loyal to the Union. Douglas Democrats, like James Spears of Bledsoe County, were generally very pro-Union as well. On the other hand, many of the old-line Whigs in White and Bledsoe Counties who backed John Bell came around to embrace the Confederacy once the war began. In some crucial ways, the social, economic and political patterns that defined antebellum Cumberland Plateau life would dictate how residents responded to the crisis of secession and war. But in other ways, the events of 1860 and 1861 would shatter old habits and relationships and plunge the Cumberland Plateau into a period of chaos and unpredictability, in which the actions of charismatic local leaders, the movement of thousands of troops and the arrival of guerrilla war would dictate the course of life and death on the plateau.

SECESSION, LOYALTY AND MOBILIZATION FOR WAR

Peter Turney, Franklin County attorney and longtime champion of Southern secession, delivered a thundering set of resolutions to the crowd gathered at the Winchester Courthouse on February 24, 1861. Two weeks earlier, Tennessee voters had chosen to remain loyal to the Union and even rejected the calling of a convention to consider the possibility of secession. The statewide vote was a "source of unfeigned mortification" to Turney and the Franklin Countians, who had hoped the state would stand "with her seven proud and gallant sisters of the South."[1] After mocking President-elect Abraham Lincoln as a "mental dwarf" who promised to "coerce" the South back into the Union, Turney's resolutions called for Franklin County to separate from Tennessee and attach itself to Alabama, "unless, before this can be done, Tennessee secede[s] from the Union, thereby giving to us a government having our consent."[2]

Just over three months later, the citizens of Scott County gathered in Huntsville to protest the state's decision, in a second referendum, to secede from the Union. On the heels of a visit from the staunchly Unionist Tennessee senator Andrew Johnson, and after rejecting secession in the June 8 referendum almost unanimously, the Scott County Court declared that the county was now the Free and Independent State of Scott. A rebellion against the rebellion, the "State of Scott" would stand under the Stars and Stripes forever.[3]

Citizens in two counties along Tennessee's Cumberland Plateau expressed polar opposite positions on the question of Tennessee's secession from the

Union, with each county vowing to secede from the state if necessary. But for most residents on the Cumberland Plateau, the secession crisis created confusion and apprehension rather than excited and committed action. The plateau occupied a space between the Union-leaning eastern Grand Division and pro-Confederate Middle Tennessee. It would be a mistake, however, to assume that loyalties followed a simple east–west axis, not to mention a divide between the northern and southern plateau. Instead, the secession crisis activated previous political and social networks while tearing apart many long-standing relationships of kin, church, party and community. Above all, the secession crisis brought chaos to the people of the Cumberland Plateau.

Several interrelated elements explain the divergent responses to secession and civil war. Preexisting political ties among plateau citizens and between those living on and off the plateau were of paramount importance. Local elites were especially important in consolidating and defending certain ideological positions, and the vast majority of middling and poor residents took their cues from these powerful neighbors.[4] There were certainly rebellious exceptions, but generally, the mass of small farmers and farm laborers looked to local leaders as exemplars of manly independence, defenders of a "way of life" and sources of aid in times of need.[5] News reached the interior communities of the plateau through these local elites, who mediated the complex events of the time through lenses that served their own interests. If a local wealthy merchant or farmer decided that the Union was the best protector of hearth, home and economy, most of his lesser-off neighbors, associates and kin would likely have concluded similarly. And if the local elite felt that the Lincoln administration imperiled the social order and threatened it with either military domination or the anarchy of emancipation, then that influential farmer was likely to convince many of his neighbors to join him in a Confederate military company when the war broke out.

There are numerous exceptions to this where ordinary people defied the will and influence of local leaders. Intra-family dynamics, personal temperament, legal troubles and simple individual conscience could yield unpredictable decisions of loyalty. And where multiple, overlapping local leaders competed for the loyalties of the people in a particular neighborhood, a vacuum in local authority appeared. These are the places where ambitious and ruthless bushwhackers, scouts, partisans and criminals became especially powerful and where residents turned to more personal, and often spiritual, sources for guidance. Still, social networks that connected the people of the Cumberland Plateau to one another and to the world beyond the plateau were most important in determining patterns of loyalty. Beyond that, social networks also influenced how people of similar loyalties responded to the war, including the mode and timing of enlistment and the sorts of acceptable responses available to a growing guerrilla war.

The first wave of decisions came with the election of the Republican Abraham Lincoln to the presidency on November 6, 1860. The Republican Party held many positions on a variety of issues, but on one issue it had united: slavery must not expand into the western territories. More ominous to Tennesseans than the Republican Party's official position was its general ideological antipathy to slavery as a permanent force in American life.[6] As such, the Republican Party never organized in Tennessee—even in the mountainous areas where slavery barely existed at all—and produced no ballots for Abraham Lincoln in the 1860 election. People on the plateau vigorously debated the merits of Northern Democrat Stephen Douglas, Southern Democrat John C. Breckinridge and the old Tennessee Whig John Bell of the Constitutional Union Party. Though all three candidates received votes around the plateau, Douglas was a distant third. A Republican victory meant that a party would control the White House with no presence in the state, no patronage network in the state, no newspaper or communication voice in the state and a worldview hostile to the growing cotton economy of the southern and southwestern parts of Tennessee.

Despite Tennessee voters' universal disapproval of Lincoln's election, very few Tennesseans thought his election was reason enough to secede from the Union. Voters felt he should be given a chance to demonstrate his fidelity to the Constitution and to the protection of slavery in the states where it existed. With non-Republicans still in control of Congress and the Supreme Court, most Tennessee voters took satisfaction that Lincoln's election would do little harm.

However, when South Carolina moved ahead with secession on December 20, 1860, followed soon after by calls to secede in the other Deep South states, Tennesseans could no longer ignore the immediate crisis. Some, like Peter Turney, had supported secession immediately after Lincoln's election, while other prominent officials, including Governor Isham Harris, thought the state should consider joining its southern neighbors in seceding from the Union. In a January 8, 1861 address to the state legislature, Harris called for a statewide referendum to approve the holding of a "sovereignty" convention and to select delegates to that convention. On February 6, voters statewide overwhelmingly chose Unionist delegates to that convention. More surprisingly, voters rejected even holding a convention, fearing that

Peter Turney, ardent secessionist from Franklin County, organized Turney's First Tennessee Regiment. *Courtesy of Tennessee State Library and Archives.*

"revolutionaries" would take the state out of the Union against the will of the majority of Tennesseans. It was the rejection of this sovereignty convention that convinced Turney and his Franklin Countians to pass resolutions joining their county to Alabama, which had already seceded on January 9. In fact, Turney was one of only three pro-secession delegates elected to the never-held convention; one of the other two was from the western section of Franklin County and the third from Lincoln County, just to the west. Turney's bailiwick proved to be more pro-secession than anywhere else in the state, including the cotton-rich counties near Memphis.[7]

For most people on the plateau, the February convention referendum was met with near-unanimous opposition, including in counties that would later come to support the Confederacy. In fact, Turney's influence seems to have been lacking in the Sequatchie Valley in the February referendum, as Marion, Sequatchie and Bledsoe Counties voted overwhelmingly for "No Convention" and for Unionist candidates.[8] The initial reporting from an election observer in Rhea County underscores the staunch Unionism of Cumberland Plateau voters. "I herewith hand you the vote of Rhea county," the observer told the editor of the *Athens Post*, "except the mountain district which will increase the Union majority."[9]

Some plateau counties like Fentress and Grundy did, in fact, support holding a convention, even though the candidates chosen from those districts were Unionist.[10] This is especially puzzling in the case of Fentress County, as that county would overwhelmingly reject secession in the June referendum. One explanation for embracing a convention may have been the partisan makeup of Fentress County, which was one of the most Democratic in the state, along with Grundy. Perhaps out of a feeling of support for the Democratic governor's convention call, Fentress voters yielded to his wish to hold a convention, even though those voters wanted that convention to reaffirm the state's commitment to the Union.

Governor Harris's January address also called for the reorganization of the moribund state militia, which would later prove essential in the creation of the Provisional Army of Tennessee, a forerunner of the Confederate Army of Tennessee. As national events headed toward a showdown at Fort Sumter in Charleston Harbor, nervous Cumberland Plateau residents continued to appeal for peace, compromise and a conservative Union. When President Lincoln called up seventy-five thousand troops to "suppress the rebellion" after the attack on Fort Sumter in April, opinions shifted dramatically in the state. For once, the majority of Tennessee's voters sided with Governor Harris, who pledged not to send a "single man for the purpose of coercion, but 50,000, if necessary, for the defense of our rights and those of our Southern brethren."[11]

Once again, Governor Harris called for a statewide referendum to determine whether Tennessee should declare independence—or "separation"—from the Federal Union and join the new Confederate States of America. Harris failed to convince many insistent Unionists that "secession" was a legitimate doctrine, which is why he appealed to the "right of revolution" that all Tennesseans would have respected. The legislature's passage of the referendum bill on May 6 allowed for the creation of the Provisional Army of Tennessee, to be used for the defense of the state and, if the referendum were approved, the Confederacy. The

Governor Isham Harris. *Courtesy of United States Library of Congress.*

date of June 8 was set for the referendum on separation from the Union and representation in the new Confederacy, and for much of Middle and West Tennessee, the outcome was foreordained.

Most Cumberland Plateau residents sifted through the question of secession like no other before it. In counties like Overton, White, Van Buren and Sequatchie, the majority of voters shifted from their "No Convention" stance in February to "Separation" in June. With support for secession in many of the westerly plateau counties reaching a fever pitch, many Union supporters decided to stay home on June 8 out of fear for their lives. "Yesterday was the great election day in Tennessee," Amanda McDowell wrote on June 9, 1861. "I guess it is voted 'out of the Union' by this time. But it would not have been had the people been allowed to vote their true sentiments. At least I do not believe it would. Nearly all the Union men in this neighborhood stayed at home, not wishing to get in a brawl and deeming it a hopeless cause."[12] Mary Sproul's father

Bethlehem United Methodist Church near Livingston. Mary Catherine Sproul recalled threats against her father for trying to invite Horace Maynard to speak.

experienced similar intimidation when planning to invite Horace Maynard to give a Union speech in Livingston. Local Confederates threatened to "riddle his hide" if Maynard were to speak, and they accused Sproul's father of being an abolitionist.[13] White County would exemplify the classic "reluctant Confederate" county of Middle Tennessee.[14]

In other plateau counties, support for the Union remained as strong as ever. Scott, Campbell and Morgan Counties went over 90 percent against secession, with Fentress and Bledsoe also giving more than 75 percent of the vote to the Union. The shift in Fentress from support for a convention in February to support for the Union in June was especially noteworthy as it defied the trend statewide. The June vote reflected a severance of partisan sentiment that had once linked the county with the Democratic Party.[15]

Another major factor in whipping up sentiment for the Union before the June 8 vote was the appearance of Senator Andrew Johnson in Jamestown, Montgomery (in Morgan County) and Huntsville. Johnson, a Democrat but a militant Unionist, was the perfect leader to encourage loyal Democrats in places like Fentress County to remain true to the Stars and Stripes. It is likely that secession sympathizers were intimidated from showing up at the polls in those counties, just as Unionists were kept away in other counties.

Ominously, the dividing line between secessionist and Union sentiment seemed to run through the western part of the Cumberland Plateau. As men and women prepared for a coming civil war, many families and communities found themselves divided along lines they might have barely noticed before. These lines often followed economic relationships, with markets linking commercial farmers and merchants of the plateau to the more pro-Confederate areas of Middle Tennessee, Alabama or Georgia. Partisan politics and patronage networks influenced people significantly as well. Tennessee's healthy two-party system, which once helped contain sectional animosities, now created yet another fault line in a state already divided over civil war.

To better judge the shift in sentiment across the plateau from the two-party tradition of antebellum Tennessee, to the secession crisis following Lincoln's election, to the outbreak of actual war after the fall of Fort Sumter, election results in five different plebiscites tell the story.[16] A gubernatorial election in 1859 between the Democrat Isham Harris and the former Whig John Netherland mostly followed the patterns of partisan voting established in the late 1830s. It offers a useful partisan baseline for plateau counties. The 1860 presidential election complicated the picture because of the split in the national Democratic Party and the centrality of national issues over the state issues that dominated the 1859 election. Still, the partisan pattern of 1859 generally dictated how plateau voters approached the presidential contest. The first major shift happened with the February 1861 referendum on holding a convention. As mentioned previously, the most permanent shift happened with the June 1861 referendum on separation. However, a fifth election held in August 1861 for the reelection of Governor Harris gives even more insight into the region's response to the state's joining of the Confederacy as, by then, any shift in sentiment was complete. By the end of August 1861, then, it was clear which Cumberland Plateau counties would most strongly support the Confederacy or the Union. It was also apparent at that point where the loyalties would remain stubbornly divided.

Table 2

ELECTION RETURNS BY COUNTY BETWEEN 1859 AND 1860
(CUMBERLAND AND PUTNAM COUNTY RETURNS NOT AVAILABLE)

COUNTY	1859 NETHERLAND (W)	1859 HARRIS (D)	1860 BELL (CU)	1860 BRECKINRIDGE (SD)	1860 DOUGLAS (ND)
Anderson	67%	33%	62%	34%	3%
Bledsoe	59%	41%	63%	31%	7%
Campbell	37%	63%	54%	43%	3%
Fentress	22%	78%	22%	75%	3%
Franklin	18%	82%	20%	77%	3%
Grundy	12%	88%	15%	85%	0%
Hamilton	51%	49%	52%	40%	8%
Marion	53%	47%	55%	39%	6%
Morgan	39%	61%	39%	50%	11%
Overton	19%	81%	21%	77%	2%
Rhea	43%	57%	41%	55%	3%
Scott	46%	54%	62%	38%	0%
Sequatchie	53%	47%	NA	NA	NA
Van Buren	40%	60%	37%	59%	4%
Warren	24%	76%	23%	76%	1%
White	53%	47%	52%	46%	2%
Plateau average	**40%**	**60%**	**41%**	**55%**	**4%**

Table 3

ELECTION RETURNS BY COUNTY IN 1861

COUNTY	FEB. 1861 NO CONVENTION	FEB. 1861 CONVENTION	JUNE 1861 NO SEPARATION	JUNE 1861 SEPARATION	1861 POLK (U)	1861 HARRIS (D)
Anderson	89%	11%	93%	7%	89%	11%
Bledsoe	77%	23%	72%	28%	69%	31%
Campbell	92%	8%	94%	6%	92%	8%
Fentress	49%	51%	84%	16%	69%	31%

County	Feb. 1861 No Convention	Feb. 1861 Convention	June 1861 No Separation	June 1861 Separation	1861 Polk (U)	1861 Harris (D)
Franklin	14%	86%	0%	100%	1%	99%
Grundy	13%	87%	2%	98%	0%	100%
Hamilton	24%	76%	60%	40%	59%	41%
Marion	87%	13%	59%	41%	57%	43%
Morgan	97%	3%	93%	7%	92%	8%
Overton	61%	39%	20%	80%	10%	90%
Rhea	88%	12%	36%	64%	31%	69%
Scott	93%	7%	96%	4%	NA	NA
Sequatchie	NA	NA	40%	60%	48%	52%
Van Buren	58%	42%	4%	96%	13%	87%
Warren	36%	64%	1%	99%	7%	93%
White	59%	41%	8%	92%	19%	81%
Plateau average	**63%**	**37%**	**41%**	**59%**	**44%**	**56%**

*Campbell, *The Attitudes of Tennesseans toward the Union*, 265–94.

With the state formally casting its support for separation from the Union in June and the subsequent addition of both the state and its army to that of the Confederacy in July, the first major wave of military enlistments on the Cumberland Plateau was for Confederate regiments. Turney's First Tennessee Volunteer Regiment was organized as early as April 1861 and immediately drew men from Franklin and surrounding counties. A sizable portion of the regiment came from upland communities, including on the edges of the plateau. Company C, recruited inside Franklin County, was known colloquially as the "Mountain Boys," while Company A, which recruited heavily from Pelham in Grundy County, was called the "Pelham Guards". The Pelham neighborhood was one of the lowest-elevation sections of Grundy County and was closest to Franklin County and Winchester. The Pelham Guards also recruited heavily from the Altamont section of Grundy County, as well as parts of Coffee and northern Franklin Counties. It included some of the most prominent men in Grundy County, including its sixty-year-old captain, Alexander Patton, who owned thirty-four slaves and was the second wealthiest man in the county after John Armfield. Other recruits in the Pelham Guards included the Northcutt brothers, Hugh

Lawson and Woodson, whose father owned nine slaves and a farm worth $11,000.[17] Organizing before Tennessee seceded from the Union, the men of Turney's First Tennessee Regiment officially enrolled in the Confederate service after they reached Virginia. Turney's First would be one of the few Tennessee units to fight the entire war in the eastern theater, a product of the men's early enthusiasm for the Confederate cause.[18]

Once Governor Harris and the state legislature passed a secession ordinance on May 6, the governor began organizing regiments into what was called, temporarily, the Provisional Army of Tennessee. It proved to be a cumbersome process to recruit, train, equip, arm and mobilize a Confederate army in Tennessee. Manpower was rarely the problem, but organization was made difficult by Harris's decision first to declare independence from the United States and then to form a "defensive league" with a Confederate government more interested in protecting its new capital at Richmond than in shoring up its western heartland. Between May 6, when the legislature adopted the secession ordinance (to be ratified on June 8), and July 31, when the Provisional Army of Tennessee was formally handed over to the Confederacy, more than twenty-five thousand Tennesseans enlisted in more than fifty regiments across the state.[19] The transfer process typically resulted in a renumbering of regiment numbers and often a consolidation with other regiments as the army passed from General Gideon Pillow's leadership to General Leonidas Polk in July and then to General Albert Sidney Johnston in September. Even after Johnston took command of all Confederate forces in the western theater—he had by then invaded and occupied much of southern Kentucky—several new regiments were formed in the fall of 1861. Many of them were formally enrolled into Confederate service while patrolling southern Kentucky, while others were placed under the command of General Felix Zollicoffer in Knoxville. The lengthy transfer of authority to Johnston, along with the politically sensitive matter of locating and constructing fortifications to guard against Federal invasion, meant that many companies and regiments would not be enrolled into official Confederate service until October 31.[20] By early 1862, when the Confederacy faced twin disasters at Mill Springs in Kentucky and Fort Donelson in Tennessee, more than seventy Tennessee regiments had been formed from all across the state, with many of them going through multiple name and number changes.

Though regiments were considered the building blocks of the army—generals would call for specific regiments to assume position in lines of battle—companies were the building blocks of regiments. Especially early in the war, companies were formed locally within neighborhoods,

Camp Myers, on a farm owned by Calvin Myers, was a Confederate Camp of Instruction for enlistees.

with captains, sergeants and lieutenants elected by the men. At full strength, regiments contained one thousand men under the leadership of a colonel, and companies included one hundred men. Occasionally, smaller groups of companies could form a battalion, formally led by a major. But Civil War companies and regiments rarely appeared in full strength, even at the beginning of the war. As time went on, casualties and desertion took their toll, and regiments often found themselves at half strength or less by the middle of the war. Additionally, men enlisted for different lengths of service, including terms of twelve months, two years, three years or the duration of the war. Constant recruitment and, after 1862, conscription meant that personnel turned over constantly. To manage this transition, armies periodically "reorganized" by consolidating, eliminating or creating units. Just as regiments were continually renamed and renumbered, companies were also reassigned and relettered. With the added complication of Tennessee's two-step process into the Confederacy—first to "independence" and then to the Confederacy proper—reorganization became a regular fact of life in the western theater of the Civil War.

One of these reorganized units was a Cumberland Plateau company, formed in the Sequatchie Valley by William D. Stewart in early September 1861. Drawing heavily from Sequatchie and northern Marion Counties, this company was first designated Company K of the Mountain Rifle Regiment of Tennessee Volunteers. When placed into a regiment at Camp Smartt in Warren County a week later, it was now called Company H of the Fifth Tennessee Provisional Army. Since another regiment in the Provisional Army from West Tennessee had already taken the Fifth Regiment number, Stewart's regiment was now titled the Thirty-fifth Regiment, Tennessee Infantry. The Thirty-fifth was not fully accepted into the Confederate States Army until October 31, when it was stationed at Bowling Green, Kentucky. Further complicating things, the Thirty-fifth was temporarily consolidated with the Forty-eighth (Nixon's) Regiment after the Battle of Chickamauga; with multiple regiments occasionally assigned the same number, adjutants added the colonel's name to the regimental title in the official records. Despite these changes, the regiment was known colloquially as either the Fifth Provisional or the Mountain Rifle Regiment. Bureaucratic renaming and renumbering meant little to the men of this regiment and company; they would continue to use the name and number they were assigned at the beginning of the war: Stewart's Company of the Tennessee Mountain Rifles or the Fifth Tennessee Provisional Army. Unlike the commanders up the hierarchical chain, Captain William D. Stewart and his Lieutenants George S. Deakins and Henry T. Kell were respected local leaders in the fertile farmland of Walnut Valley in eastern Sequatchie County. The company, and its name, thus represented the Confederate-supporting leaders of that community throughout the war.

Most Confederate companies recruited along the Cumberland Plateau were formed in the summer of 1861 and, like Stewart's Company of

Sequatchie County, typically drew from single neighborhoods. But the timing is as important as the location. Many of the leaders in the earlier companies had supported secession from the beginning and enlisted in provisional units before the June 8 referendum. For example, Company C, later reorganized as Company K, of the Sixteenth Tennessee Infantry, recruited heavily from the New Ark and Cassville sections of northern and western White County. Though the 1860 census listed Captain Daniel T. Brown as an older man of modest means, Company C drew from a cross-section of middle-class merchants and commercial farmers in the heart of White County. Brown himself enlisted as early as May 20, 1861; was wounded at Perryville in October 1862; was captured and sent to Camp Chase until April 1863; then was transferred to Fort Delaware; and was released on April 25, 1863. After his release, Brown was promoted to lieutenant colonel of the Sixteenth Regiment in May 1863. Though Brown moved up the Confederate military ranks, New Ark and Cassville boys would fill out the ranks of Company C/K to the very end. For example, William Turlington, a clerk living in the household of grocer S.D. Price in New Ark, enlisted the same day as Brown and was later promoted to captain, serving the rest of the war in Company K. Soldiers in Company K were of varying levels of wealth and status. Some, like the literary student Polk Fancher, were sons of elite slaveholders, while others, like James M. Smith, were struggling, poor farmers living in large non-slaveholding households with wealth under $300. Both enlisted in May 1861 and came from Cassville, however, and likely knew each other before the war began. Either way, considering how early the company was formed, it is likely that these men were among the strongest secessionists of White County.[21]

In the summer of 1861, after Tennessee officially seceded on June 8, several Confederate enlistment camps appeared either on or adjacent to the plateau, including Camp Smartt near McMinnville in Warren County, Camps Zollicoffer and Myers in Overton County and Camp McGinnis in Fentress County. Other units formed at Camp Cummings in Knoxville or Camp Trousdale, known officially as the Camp of Instruction, in Sumner County. It was at these sites that men from the plateau officially enlisted in either Provisional Army of Tennessee or permanent Confederate Army of Tennessee companies and regiments, received training and drilling and were placed into brigades and divisions for service.

Enthusiasm for the Confederate cause along the western edge of the Cumberland Plateau in the summer of 1861 resulted in the creation of several companies at these induction camps, with most of the companies led by prominent prewar merchants, lawyers and other town-based

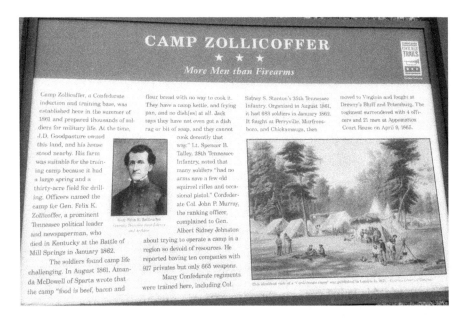

Camp Zollicoffer in Overton County.

professionals. First cousins George Stewart Deakins and William Deakins Stewart formed Company K/H of the aforementioned Thirty-fifth Tennessee, the company composed mostly of men from Sequatchie County. George Deakins was an attorney in Jasper in Marion County shortly before the war, and his cousin William was a middling farmer in Sequatchie County with one slave. The cousins joined fellow Sequatchie County farmer (and also owner of one slave) Henry Kell and a teacher from DeKalb County named Levi L. Dearman to form a company in the Provisional Army's First Tennessee Mountain Rifle Regiment. Upon reaching Camp Smartt in Warren County in September 1861, the unit was placed under the command of Colonel Benjamin J. Hill and given the designation Company K of the Fifth Tennessee Volunteer Regiment.

In Bledsoe County, where Unionist sentiment still dominated in the summer of 1861, a network of commercial farmers centered on John Bridgeman of Pikeville rushed to join a regiment known as the Tulloss Rangers, named in honor of the unit's benefactor, James Tulloss.[22] Early recruits in the Tulloss Rangers include many interlocking elites of Bledsoe County, such as the Worthingtons, Greers, Thurmans and Billingsleys. In the southern precincts of Cumberland County, which had been a part of Bledsoe County until 1855, the Tulloss Rangers attracted recruits as well. Thomas Sherrill, son of

Cumberland County sheriff Cravens Sherrill, joined the Tulloss Rangers in the summer of 1861. Notably, his younger brother Samuel joined a different unit organized a few months later—one that included mostly Cumberland County men. The elder brother's network around Devilstep Hollow and Ormes Store in southern Cumberland County extended into Bledsoe County and the Sequatchie Valley. He was a Tulloss Ranger, and the Tulloss Rangers included his social network. Perhaps reflecting the growth of the new Cumberland County, the younger son of the sheriff attached himself to a company known regionally as the "Cumberland County Confederates." For the younger Samuel, he served as part of the new social network of Cumberland County elites, and Company A of the Twenty-eight Tennessee Consolidated Infantry was the proving ground for membership. The Tulloss Rangers were eventually organized as Company F in the Fourth Tennessee Cavalry (Branner's) and then consolidated with another unit to form Company F of the Second Tennessee Cavalry Battalion (Ashby's). But they would remain the Tulloss Rangers in common parlance throughout the war.

Willis Scott Bledsoe, an attorney in Jamestown, formed one of the most respected Confederate "partisan" companies in the Upper Cumberland,

John Bridgeman House, Pikeville. Bridgeman organized the Tulloss Rangers. Union troops occupied and ransacked the house in June 1862 and recruited Unionists nearby.

with his family and business associates in Fentress and Overton Counties at the core of what became known as Scott Bledsoe's Independent Cavalry. Scott Bledsoe enlisted in the Confederate service at Camp McGinnis near Travisville in August 1861. His cavalry unit was officially formed at Camp Myers in the Monroe area of Overton County and guarded the state line over the following months. A year later, Bledsoe's Cavalry would be designated Company I of the Fourth Tennessee Cavalry (Murray's) during a reorganization after the Battle of Perryville in October 1862. It would serve both in conventional service and in a guerrilla capacity throughout the war. And like other units on the plateau, the company would continue to be known by the personage of its organizer and leader, Scott Bledsoe.

Interestingly, one of Bledsoe's first recruits was a client of his, under indictment for the murder of James Reed, a Fentress County constable in 1858. The defendant in the case, though a native of heavily Unionist Clinton County, Kentucky, had convinced himself that by joining Bledsoe's Confederate cavalry company, all charges would be dropped. That defendant was none other than Champ Ferguson, a man who would come to define the extreme brutality and violence of the guerrilla war along the Cumberland Plateau.[23] Most of the men who joined Bledsoe, however, were respected merchants, professionals and commercial farmers in Fentress and Overton Counties and were armed early on with navy repeater pistols. Camp McGinnis bustled with activity in the late summer of 1861, with as many as ten thousand men appearing to enlist, train, drill and pass the time. The full bureaucratic sorting out of company and regimental names would take time, but the company cohesion that pulled together men from Overton and Fentress Counties in Tennessee and Clinton County in Kentucky would persist.

More conventional Confederate companies formed at Camp Zollicoffer and Myers in Overton County, Camp Smartt in Warren County and Camp Harris near Tullahoma in Franklin County. Three companies from White Company, all organized in the Twenty-fifth Tennessee Infantry, reveal the networks of kin and neighborhood that influenced the leadership selection process. James Snodgrass, captain of Company A, was a physician, while William Gooch Smith, captain of Company C, lived in a household with a schoolteacher in southern White County. The leadership and enlistment roll of Company E includes men of all income levels from the Cherry Creek community north of Sparta.[24]

Most of these Tennessee Confederates earnestly believed that they were engaging in a fight to protect their homes and communities from Federal invasion. Until late August, Governor Harris and Generals Gideon Pillow and Leonidas Polk maintained the illusion that a neutral Kentucky would act as a buffer against a direct invasion of Tennessee. More menacing in their eyes was a potential naval assault down the Mississippi River, with Memphis a prime target. Fearing an imminent invasion from Cairo, Illinois, General Polk invaded Kentucky and seized the bluffs at Columbus, Kentucky. Polk rightly claimed that Unionists had already violated Kentucky neutrality by raising pro-Union regiments at Camp Dick Robinson, near where the Wilderness Road meets the Central Kentucky Railroad. But the majority of Kentuckians, then leaning toward the Union, saw things differently. They viewed Polk's invasion as a violation of Kentucky's neutrality and a cause for joining officially with the Union. The invasion proved to be a Confederate disaster for military and political reasons. Shortly before the legislature made the Union move official, Federal general Ulysses Grant invaded and occupied Paducah and threatened a further invasion of West Tennessee. General Albert Sidney Johnston, now in charge of all Confederate forces in the West, pushed deeper into Kentucky and established a defensive line along an arc from Cumberland Gap in the east to the Mississippi River in the west and passing through Bowling Green, where Simon Bolivar Buckner commanded Confederate forces in Johnston's center.[25]

Felix Zollicoffer was placed in command of Tennessee's military forces in the east, tasked with the responsibility of recruiting and training more young men for the Confederate army, establishing a defensible line in southern Kentucky, wooing stubborn Unionists in East Tennessee to support the Confederacy and preventing Federal soldiers in Kentucky from sending arms to Unionists in East Tennessee.[26] Zollicoffer was generally successful in his efforts to raise and train troops in the northwestern part of the plateau, with hundreds of men enlisting at Camps Zollicoffer, Myers and McGinnis.

By the end of September, the Confederacy seemed in firm military control of the state as far east as the Sequatchie Valley in the south and the Wolf River in the north. In addition, the Confederate army had established what it believed to be firm control of the Tennessee Valley, from Chattanooga and Washington in Hamilton and Rhea Counties in the southern valley, through Knoxville and up into the Holston Valley. Still, the gaps in the Cumberland Mountains and Plateau made Zollicoffer nervous. It was easy enough to secure Cumberland Gap and prevent a full-scale Federal invasion there. But Rogers Gap, Baptist Gap, Big Creek Gap and Wheelers Gap were equally passable invasion routes for a Federal force, and Zollicoffer knew plenty well

Felix Zollicoffer, in military command over East Tennessee
early in the war, was killed at the Battle of Mill Springs in
January 1862. *Courtesy of United States Library of Congress.*

that the Federal army in Kentucky would seek a way to rescue Tennessee
Unionists from Confederate occupation. Adding to Zollicoffer's worries
were two other points of entry west of Wheeler's Gap: north of Jamestown
and near Celina along the Cumberland River. This long stretch of rugged
terrain would witness the first major military action on the Cumberland
Plateau: the Affair at Travisville.

More significant than the Travisville incursion were political events in
the state, which culminated in a failed sabotage campaign and a massive
suppression of dissent. As communities along the western edge of the
plateau came around to support the Confederate war effort in the spring
and summer of 1861, most of the counties along the northern and eastern

sections of the plateau continued to resist the Confederate tide. Before the June 8 referendum, Unionists met at Knoxville to consider options in the event of an expected vote for secession. Delegates came from across East Tennessee and included plateau counties. Following the referendum, the delegates met again at Greeneville. After mulling armed insurrection, the delegates petitioned Governor Harris for separate statehood for East Tennessee. Some delegates decided to take action on their own. Robert K. Byrd, a slaveholding Unionist from Roane County, met with Ephraim Langley and Samuel Honeycutt of Morgan County and Joseph Cooper of Campbell County and secretly planned to raise companies in their own counties.[27] These men would compose the elements of the First Tennessee Volunteer Infantry Regiment (USA), or First East Tennessee Regiment. Cooper's company was designated Company A, making his unit the perfect counter to Alexander Patton's Company A of Turney's First Infantry, CSA. These two Cumberland Plateau companies were among the first raised in the state for each side.

Not surprisingly, the Confederate governor ignored the request for separate statehood and worked to build up support for his government as he ran for reelection against William H. Polk, brother of former president James K. Polk. Harris, concerned as ever about securing reelection, treated East Tennessee loyalists gingerly, despite demands from Confederate supporters that he suppress the "Tory" element. In a confirmation of the June 8 vote, most East Tennessee and eastern Cumberland Plateau counties voted for Polk as a protest against Harris's Confederate policy on August 1. Once Harris secured reelection, he began to crack down against so-called Tories in the east, arresting T.A.R. Nelson and threatening to confiscate arms. On the day after the reelection of Governor Harris, Joseph Cooper enlisted in the Federal army for ninety-day service at Jacksboro.[28]

In the next week, hundreds of other Cumberland Plateau Unionists joined companies formed by men like Sam Honeycutt, a teacher from Morgan County and Greeneville Convention delegate; John W. Bowman and Amos Marney, both small farmers of the Wrightsville section of Roane County; and Mitchell Millsaps, a farmer from Jamestown.[29] Bowman and Marney commanded Company A and recruited men from throughout Roane County, while Mitchell Millsaps and James Melton enlisted men from northern Morgan and Fentress Counties into what became Company B of the Second East Tennessee Infantry Regiment. Officially organized at Camp Dick Robinson, the Second Tennessee, under the command of Colonel James Carter, had added a company of men from Anderson County and

Sam Honeycutt's Company D, raised in Morgan and Cumberland Counties, by September 1.[30]

As men from the northeastern plateau slipped into Kentucky to join the First and Second Tennessee Regiments, General Zollicoffer worked to tighten the noose around this belt of Toryism. Paramilitary raids from Unionists within Tennessee and from Kentucky, many of them armed with little more than squirrel guns, alerted Confederate authorities to the possibility of a large-scale Federal invasion of East Tennessee in the fall of 1861. Continuing in the weeks after the Travisville Affair of late September, small bands of pro-Union guerrillas attacked Confederate supply lines and harassed recruiters en route to Knoxville. As the Confederates pushed into Kentucky and established a forward line of defense, Confederate civilians warned of an increase of these Unionist attacks behind the lines. It appeared to most observers that Zollicoffer's men, then heading northwest out of Cumberland Gap on the Wilderness Road to stop Federal recruitment at Camp Dick Robinson, would soon clash with the growing body of Union soldiers gathering at that enlistment camp. On September 18, Zollicoffer's men encountered a Federal camp known as Camp Andy Johnson near Barbourville, where Cooper and Byrd had organized most of the First Regiment in August. Zollicoffer defeated a valiant but overmatched unit of pro-Union Kentucky Home Guards, which retreated to the northwest toward the Rockcastle Hills.[31]

Union general George Thomas, recently placed in command, moved south out of Camp Dick Robinson and established a well-fortified stronghold on a natural rock bluff that he called Camp Wildcat. With Thomas were several East Tennesseans hoping to return to their native state to destroy the East Tennessee and Virginia Railroad and lead a Unionist rebellion against the occupying Confederates. Sandstone caprock atop a bluff that had eroded over millions of years provided the Federal soldiers a better rampart of protection than the sturdiest fortress constructed by man. Nevertheless, Zollicoffer continued northward from Barbourville, hoping to capture this natural fortification before Union soldiers could establish their position. On October 21, Zollicoffer's men charged the bluff at Camp Wildcat only to be repelled by regiments from Indiana, Ohio and Kentucky, with the East Tennessee Unionists largely in reserve. Zollicoffer retreated back to Tennessee, only to attempt a much larger assault eighty miles to the west in January.

Thomas considered pursuit through Cumberland Gap, an invasion that could coincide with a spectacular railroad sabotage plot set for November 8. With the approval of President Lincoln, Andrew Johnson and the secretary of war, Simon Cameron, Unionists led by brothers William and Samuel Carter of Upper East Tennessee were to burn the bridges of the East Tennessee and Virginia and East Tennessee and Georgia Railroads with the hopes of severing rail links between Virginia and the rest of the Confederacy. The defeat of Zollicoffer at Camp Wildcat made for perfect timing—or so Carter and the bridge burners thought. But the commander in charge of all Kentucky operations, Robert Anderson of Fort Sumter fame, had recently fallen ill and was replaced by William Tecumseh Sherman. After conferring with other generals, Sherman decided that a better invasion path into the Confederacy would go through Middle Tennessee, with an attack on Nashville by either the Louisville and Nashville Railroad via Bowling Green or down the Cumberland River after seizing Fort Donelson. As for East Tennessee, Sherman felt it would be a death trap, with muddy winter roads and an inadequate food supply.[32]

Zollicoffer took no chances. After the defeat at Camp Wildcat, he retreated south through Cumberland Gap and Powell's Valley to Jacksboro, leaving a battalion of Alabamians to guard Cumberland Gap and hoping generally to "to try to intercept the enemy before he descends the mountain."[33] But which mountain would the Federal army descend? With the gaps on Cumberland Mountain east of Jacksboro sufficiently plugged by Zollicoffer's men, the most obvious and vulnerable invasion route would be from Monticello or Albany, Kentucky, into Fentress County and then southeastward through Scott, Morgan and Anderson or Roane Counties toward the Tennessee River and its vulnerable railroad bridges. Zollicoffer had received conflicting reports of thousands of Union soldiers waiting just a few miles north of the state line and heading for Jamestown. Confederate senator Landon Carter Haynes similarly reported to President Jefferson Davis the immediate "danger of invasion by the Lincoln forces of East Tennessee by way of Jamestown, Fentress County, Tennessee."[34] Unable to reach Jamestown from Jacksboro, Zollicoffer decided to concentrate his forces at Winters Gap, a vital crossroads at the foot of Walden's Ridge.

Fortunately for Zollicoffer, Sherman called off Thomas's planned invasion of Tennessee. It was devastating news for East Tennessee Unionists that they would not be going back to liberate their homes. Even worse, the news never reached the bridge burners, who went ahead and set fire to five bridges. Sherman's assessment was probably correct militarily, as a Middle Tennessee campaign was more likely to open up the entire Confederate heartland to Federal occupation. But because word of his change of plans never reached the bridge burners, the saboteurs were easily identified and arrested after destroying four bridges.

What started as an abrupt turn toward suppression of Toryism after Harris's reelection in August now became a full-on crackdown against all Union sympathizers in East Tennessee. From November 8 on, the Confederate national government and Isham Harris's state government treated the people of East Tennessee as disloyal Tories to be disarmed and placed under martial law. Confederates in East Tennessee were even more outraged at the behavior of their Unionist neighbors. Colonel Danville Ledbetter, placed in command of all troops in charge of "protection of the railroad from Bristol to Chattanooga," initiated a brutal crackdown against Unionist sympathizers.[35] The stream of Tennessee Union sympathizers fleeing to Kentucky now became a flood as tens of thousands searched for safe routes out of the state in order to join rapidly forming Federal units that would, someday, liberate their homelands.

Dan Ellis, the Old Red Fox, piloted thousands of Union supporters to Kentucky. *Ellis,* Thrilling Adventures of Daniel Ellis, *frontispiece.*

Pro-Union civilians throughout the plateau served as scouts, guiding men to Kentucky to join the Federal army. This "Union Underground Railroad" ferried thousands of Tennesseans through the most rugged sections of the plateau to avoid Confederate conscription agents and guerrillas. Daniel Ellis, a guide from Carter County, shepherded approximately four thousand Unionists from across East Tennessee into Kentucky. Known as the Old Red Fox, Ellis made twenty expeditions and used every gap and hollow in the Cumberland Plateau to ferry his charges to safety.[36] An equally colorful guide was Richard Flynn of Cumberland County. With a network reaching Hamilton County, Richard Flynn and his wife, Ezylphia, guided hundreds to Kentucky from southeastern Tennessee.[37]

Perhaps more important than the legendary men who guided the "Tory exiles" to Kentucky were the women and girls who gave shelter, food, directions and protection to the hunted Union men. In a war increasingly

Richard and Ezylphia Flynn piloted Unionists from Devilstep Hollow toward Kentucky.

marked by households pitted against one another in a treacherous landscape, women offered a critical supply line for male civilians and soldiers alike. Long after the war, Nancy Lowe told of an elaborate network through which her aunt Polly Hand guided as many as fifty men in a single night to Kentucky from Devilstep Hollow, where the Sequatchie River emerges from a spring in southern Cumberland County. As Nancy Lowe put it, "Aunt Polly done as much to help the Union win the war as the men in uniform."[38]

Though the Union army never launched its great liberation campaign for East Tennessee, Colonels Thomas Bramlette and Frank Wolford of Kentucky continued to menace Confederate camps McGinnis and Myers, causing Confederates to flee a potential invasion. Through an informant in the land closely divided in sentiment, Bramlette learned of the Confederates' flight south and west past Livingston to Camp Zollicoffer. The Confederates returned to Camp McGinnis after discovering that the invasion was called off and having "recover[ed] from their fright and venture[d] to peep out this side of their brush."[39] Bramlette reported to General Thomas, "I know their hiding place, and how to surround it, when they get sufficient confidence to think themselves safe."[40]

Zollicoffer tried once again to push back against advancing Federal positions by concentrating his forces near the Cumberland River at Mill

Springs just west of Somerset, where he hoped to resume the offensive toward Camp Dick Robinson in the spring. George Thomas moved south from Camp Dick Robinson to Logan's Crossroads, hoping to trap Zollicoffer on the north bank of the Cumberland. Union general Albin Schoepf at Somerset planned to cross Fishing Creek and join Thomas's men. Schoepf arrived in time to take the advantage on the battlefield. The dreary rain and fog shrouding the battlefield near Mill Springs on January 19, 1862, led to confusion from the beginning. At one point, Zollicoffer mistakenly entered a camp of Kentucky Unionists and was quickly recognized and shot dead. George Crittenden took field command (he was technically Zollicoffer's superior) until Thomas's men broke through the Confederate lines and forced a stampede of retreat south and west into Tennessee.[41] Many Cumberland Plateau–based regiments saw action at Mill Springs, including the Twenty-

Military activity along Cumberland Mountain. *Maps accompanying* OR.

fifth Tennessee. Once back in Tennessee, the Confederates camped at Gainesboro in Jackson County before moving as far as Murfreesboro. Mill Springs would prove to be an unmitigated disaster for the Confederacy in the western theater. It meant the collapse of the Confederacy's hold on eastern Kentucky and the potential loss of Cumberland Gap.

Once again, rumors of a Federal invasion along the plateau drew the attention of Confederate commanders. Colonel Danville Ledbetter, charged with defending the railroad and trying desperately to maintain authority in East Tennessee generally, reported increasing Unionist guerrilla activity in Scott, Morgan and Campbell Counties. The attacks from "traitors" led by a "Captain Duncan" were significant enough to reroute Confederate cavalry away from Crittenden's larger force.

No invasion was planned for East Tennessee or the Cumberland Plateau, however—at least, not so soon after Mill Springs. Confederate guerrillas would take up the fight as disgruntled Confederates retreated into Tennessee and emboldened Unionists sought the advantage. For the people of the Cumberland Plateau, the period following the Battle of Mill Springs would bring all the horrors of both conventional and guerrilla war to their doorsteps. For the next several months, conventional war shifted well to the west. General Grant and Admiral Foote launched a combined naval and land assault on the forts guarding the lower Tennessee and Cumberland Rivers just days after the skirmishing in Morgan County. The successful Union capture of Forts Henry and Donelson and the subsequent fall of Nashville to the Union army permanently changed the dynamics of war in Tennessee. For the next year and a half, the Cumberland Plateau would define the boundary between pro-Confederate but Union-occupied Middle Tennessee and pro-Union but still Confederate-occupied East Tennessee. The Cumberland Plateau was now truly "No Man's Land."

4

ARMIES IN MOTION

C olonel Henry Hambright of the Seventy-ninth Pennsylvania Infantry wrote a glowing report of the conduct of his men as they "continued their march over the Cumberland Mountains, arriving before Chattanooga on the 7th after a long and tedious march."[1] After days of scattering pickets in the Sequatchie Valley, routing a small Rebel force in Sweedens Cove and cannonading entrenched positions on the south banks of the Tennessee River, Hambright's commanding general, James A. Negley, commented, "I do not consider the capture of Chattanooga as very difficult or hazardous, if we were prepared to do it and then hold the place."[2] Confederate major general Edmund Kirby Smith, commanding East Tennessee from Knoxville, concurred. Chattanooga was vulnerable, and Smith's "little force" was "entirely inadequate to hold the department."[3]

Negley turned back from Chattanooga without seizing the Gateway to the Deep South due to "our limited supplies, and the fact that our expedition has accomplished all we expected to do."[4] On his way back over the Cumberland Plateau and through the Sequatchie Valley, Negley boasted, "The Union people in East Tennessee are wild with joy. They meet us along the roads by hundreds."[5] Negley promised to military governor Andrew Johnson, "I shall send you a number of their principal persecutors from the Sequatchie Valley."[6] A relieved General Smith simply noted, "General Mitchel retired from Chattanooga…His force evacuated…about 7,000 effective…evacuated Sequatchie Valley yesterday and recrossed the mountain into Middle Tennessee."[7]

And so passed by a great opportunity to capture Chattanooga in June 1862, the same month that the Army of the Potomac failed to take the Confederate capital at Richmond. Historians have long wondered what effect an early capture of Chattanooga would have meant for the course of the war, especially as Union general George W. Morgan subsequently secured Cumberland Gap and would have forced the evacuation of an encircled E. Kirby Smith and the Confederate army from all of East Tennessee.[8] As it turns out, it would take nearly eighteen more bloody months for the Union army to take and hold Chattanooga for good.

Why did Negley not take the city in June 1862? And why did it take so long to accomplish this strategic objective? The answer has much to do with poor leadership from Union general Don Carlos Buell, who moved at such a leisurely pace across northern Alabama after the capture of the vital railroad crossroads at Corinth, Mississippi, in late May 1862. Ever worried about his long supply line back to Louisville, Kentucky, and unwilling to forage heavily on the citizens of the region, Buell limped along gingerly, only to find that the just-defeated Confederate army had taken the rails south through Mississippi and back up through Alabama in time to reach Chattanooga by early August. By then, Braxton Bragg, in one of his few successful ventures as a commander, prepared to launch a surprising invasion of Kentucky by crossing the Cumberland Plateau, with E. Kirby Smith leading a parallel column north out of Knoxville to Lexington.[9]

More important than hesitant leadership, however, was the reality of the Cumberland Plateau's topography. It was one thing to capture Chattanooga, which lay in a bowl between the ridges to the east and the plateau to the west.[10] It was another thing to hold it, as even Negley admitted. The maze of gaps, ridges, gorges and hollows made the supply and defense of Chattanooga exceedingly difficult. Invading armies could shield their movements behind impenetrable rock faces. The imposing bluffs surrounding the city—Missionary Ridge to the east, Signal Mountain to the northwest, Raccoon Mountain to the west and Lookout Mountain to the south—made for perfect siege operations. And the great logistical paths that made Chattanooga so important a city in the first place—the Tennessee River and three long-distance railroads—were nearly impossible to secure. From June 1862 until November 1863, Chattanooga, the crossroads of the South and the "funnel of the universe," would remain an elusive target and a death trap.[11]

Though geography figured heavily into every Civil War battle in some form or another, it is hard to think of another series of military campaigns during the Civil War more dependent on the peculiarities of geography

View of Chattanooga from Signal Mountain. The city is a "bowl" surrounded by mountains and the "funnel of the universe."

than the Kentucky invasion of 1862; the Tullahoma campaign of mid-1863; and the Chickamauga, Chattanooga and Knoxville campaigns in the fall of 1863. The people of the Cumberland Plateau saw their once-remote farms and homesteads turned into disease-ridden military camps, army supply depots, makeshift hospitals and killing fields. Men and women sometimes guided troops to their destinations and at other times deceived or resisted them. In the midst of this intensifying war in the western theater, Confederate and Union armies turned to conscription to fill out the ranks. Legions of ordinary people sought refuge from conscription agents, cavalry forces scouring the region for food and guerrilla forces that filled in the vacuum of authority. The No Man's Land from Cumberland Gap to the Tennessee River Gorge and from Jamestown to Chattanooga would emerge as the front line of the Civil War in the western theater between the summer of 1862 and the end of 1863.

At first, events in the winter and early spring of 1862 portended a military collapse for the Rebels. A month after the Battle of Mill Springs, Union forces under General Ulysses Grant launched a full invasion of Tennessee along the Tennessee and Cumberland Rivers west of Clarksville. The Battle of Fort Donelson and the surrender of thirteen thousand Confederate troops led to the evacuation of Nashville and, a few weeks later, the appointment of Andrew Johnson as the new military governor of Tennessee. Unionists on the Cumberland Plateau rejoiced at this turn of events and continued to relish Federal victories at Shiloh and Corinth in April 1862.

With Grant pressing southward along the Tennessee River and Buell securing the defenses of Nashville, the Federal army set its sights on the railroad crossing at Corinth, Mississippi. Confederate forces under General Albert Sidney Johnston moved south from Nashville to Alabama and west to Corinth. Johnston advanced north from Corinth, hoping to destroy Grant's Army of the Tennessee near Pittsburg Landing before Buell's Army of the Ohio reinforcements arrived. Critical delays proved fatal for Johnston, as Buell's men rescued Grant's brave but reeling troops on the night of April 6, 1862.[12] Meanwhile, Johnston was killed during that first day at the Battle of Shiloh, with Governor Isham Harris at his side. The next day, Buell and Grant drove the Confederate Army of Tennessee, now under P.G.T. Beauregard, from the field and back into Mississippi. A slow and methodical advance on Corinth led to a siege and surrender of the town to Buell in late May. The Confederate forces retreated farther south, and Buell eyed his great—and ultimately lost—opportunity to move east along the Memphis and Charleston Railroad and secure the vital city of Chattanooga. General Negley's brief cannonade of Chattanooga on June 8 was the only threat the Federals would muster.

For the people of the Cumberland Plateau, the defeat of Confederate forces at Mill Springs, Fort Donelson and Shiloh meant that pro-Confederate areas to the west of the plateau would fall under closer occupation by the Federal army and the military governorship of Andrew Johnson. In the east, however, E. Kirby Smith was placed in command from Knoxville and worked to build a Confederate military presence in the region, despite the sentiments of much of the population.

Smith spent the next few months fighting off external invading forces while trying, in vain, to suppress pro-Union support for a liberating force from Kentucky. Leaving Boston, Kentucky (just north of Jellico, Tennessee), on March 10, Union general James P. Carter of the Second East Tennessee Infantry invaded Campbell County and hoped to secure Big Creek Gap, where "rebel forces…[were] molesting the persons and property of Union citizens."[13] Carter's Second Tennessee was not the only regiment to make the advance into the state. Joseph Cooper's Company A of the First Tennessee also joined the campaign, making this one of the first sustained efforts by East Tennessee and Cumberland Plateau Unionists to liberate their homelands. With Kentucky Cavalry to lead the way through the dense forest, Cooper, the Campbell Countian, led his men on a nine-mile march "with superhuman exertion" over Cumberland Mountain to meet and surround the Confederates guarding Big Creek Gap. After routing a small Confederate detachment, Cooper and Carter captured Jacksboro and then sent a cavalry detachment out to destroy one thousand pounds of saltpeter and eleven thousand pounds of bacon. The people living there, who were "truly loyal in their sentiments and hailed our troops with unbounded enthusiasm," made the march into Powell Valley easier.[14] A frustrated Smith complained, "The entire population of these counties is hostile to us, those able to bear arms being regularly organized as Home Guards." Smith was convinced that the success at Big Creek Gap and Jacksboro was the result of "treachery," not just of the citizens there but also of the Confederate force guarding the gap. Smith accused Confederate soldiers from East Tennessee and the Cumberland Mountains of holding "strong Union proclivities, greatly increased by their near relationship to and from intimate association with many citizens who have fled the country and espoused the Federal cause."[15]

Carter and Cooper were ordered to retreat back to Flat Lick, Kentucky, but they had sent a message to Smith and the Confederate high command that control of the Cumberland Mountains would require a much heavier hand. In response, General E. Kirby Smith sent General Ledbetter and Colonel Vaughn's Third Tennessee Infantry from Kingston up into Morgan, Campbell and Scott Counties "for the purpose of dispersing organized Federal bands existing there," as well as to remove supplies that could be made available to a potential invading Union force.[16]

The Confederate general reiterated his frustration: "All

Union general Joseph A. Cooper of Campbell County.

loyal citizens have been expelled from the country."[17] There were not likely many "loyal" citizens—to the Confederacy—in Scott and Campbell Counties to begin with. But the few who were there could no longer subsist in this "Tory" hotbed.

General E. Kirby Smith placed most of East Tennessee, including much of the Cumberland Plateau, under formal martial law on April 8, with President Jefferson Davis suspending the writ of habeas corpus. For the next fourteen months, Smith and his successors used a combination of stringent and lenient policies designed to separate ordinary citizens from the influence of their mostly Unionist leaders. "The arrest of the leading men in every county, and their incarceration South, may bring these people right," Smith relayed to Adjutant General Samuel Cooper.[18] Understanding the power of local leadership among such an "ignorant, primitive people, completely in the hands of, and under the guidance of, their leaders," Smith sought to reconcile the local population to Confederate rule while sending the leading Unionists to jails in Georgia. The remaining local leaders would be required to swear oaths of loyalty to the Confederacy. Smith also expelled the families of leading Unionists and threatened to expel the families of soldiers who went to Kentucky to join the Union army. To mollify the pro-Union citizens, General Smith exempted East Tennessee from the Confederate Conscription Act issued in April and offered general amnesty to Union soldiers who swore an oath to the Confederacy within thirty days. Ever concerned that existing East Tennessee Confederate units, including the Fourth Tennessee, were disloyal to the Confederacy, Smith sent them to Georgia. Presumably, newer recruits, no longer under the influence of treacherous Tory leaders, would be more reliable in guarding the gaps of Cumberland Mountain and keeping order. A smaller group of noncombat "sappers and miners" near Cumberland Gap would remain, though many of them had been present at Big Creek Gap in March.[19]

The Union army in eastern Kentucky continued to threaten invasion of East Tennessee in the late spring and early summer of 1862. General George W. Morgan of the Union Army of the Ohio occupied a position close to Cumberland Gap by May 1862. He planned a feint at Cumberland Gap while sending General Spears, a native of Bledsoe County, through Rogers Gap, which was a small bridle path between Cumberland and Big Creek Gaps.[20] As Smith reinforced Big Creek and Cumberland Gaps, Morgan authorized a militant Unionist from Hamilton County named William Clift to form a new partisan regiment from Scott and Morgan Counties "to annoy the enemy's rear."[21] Beginning in early June, Morgan sent Colonel John DeCourcy through

Rogers Gap to clear out obstructions left by Zollicoffer and open a clearer path into Powells Valley. As Negley and Ormsby Mitchel threatened to take Chattanooga, General Smith decided that removing General Carter Stevenson and his brigade at Cumberland Gap and sending them to Chattanooga would better serve him. By June 18, the campaign of feints and maneuvers through complex terrain had resulted in the abandonment of the "Gibraltar of the West" to Union general George W. Morgan.

The problem of supply would bedevil General George Morgan at Cumberland Gap just as it did Confederate general Stevenson and Colonel Rains before them. This was true for the rest of the Cumberland Mountains and Plateau as well. Guns and ammunition were difficult to deliver, even though the raw material to make gunpowder—saltpeter—was found in abundance. The process of transporting military stores and food supplies proved exceedingly difficult. Valleys like the Powell and Sequatchie were rich with agricultural produce and pork, and commanders turned quickly to forage for support. But as historian Earl Hess has emphasized, the main obstacle facing Union commanders in the western theater was the logistical challenge of supplying an army spread out over vast stretches of territory.[22]

Henry Halleck, a famously cautious and studious career army officer, was placed in command of all Union forces in the West after Shiloh. His deliberate march to Corinth secured that city without a major battle. He planned a similarly cautious march across northern Alabama to Chattanooga, securing supply lines in anticipation of a future offensive into Georgia. Buell traveled east along the Memphis and Charleston Railroad from Corinth to Huntsville, Alabama, with forty thousand men in six divisions. Alexander McDowell McCook and Thomas L. Crittenden continued to Battle Creek in Marion County, past the junction at Stevenson where the Nashville and Chattanooga and the Memphis and Charleston Railroads met. Thomas Wood and George Thomas stayed on the west side of the plateau at Decherd in Franklin County, where they guarded the Nashville and Chattanooga Railroad before it headed through the Cowan Tunnel toward Stevenson. On the left or northern point, William Nelson occupied McMinnville, with one of Thomas's brigades at Pelham, in between McMinnville and Decherd. On a sixty-mile line that traversed the Cumberland Plateau, Buell posted sentinels along three different railroads: the Nashville and Chattanooga, the Nashville and Decatur and the Memphis and Charleston.[23] Any action ahead of the sixty-mile line, like Negley's approach to Chattanooga on June 8, would have to be pulled back until supply lines could be fully established and protected.

Sensing Buell's vulnerability, Nathan Bedford Forrest launched a surprising cavalry raid against Union positions in Murfreesboro and against rail bridges at Nashville in late July.[24] On August 12, John Hunt Morgan launched another cavalry raid northeast of Nashville, destroying the Big South Tunnel near Gallatin and forcing Buell's men to go on half rations while repairs were made.[25] These cavalry raids, from leaders who were not yet household names, set back Buell's advance several weeks. Meanwhile, the newly named Confederate Army of the Mississippi, now under the command of Braxton Bragg, traveled by rail from Tupelo, Mississippi, to Mobile, Alabama; up to Atlanta, Georgia; and then up to Chattanooga by the end of July.[26] Crowds cheered the Confederate troops in transit across the rails of the Deep South. Confederate conscription significantly enhanced the size of Bragg's army, which arrived in Chattanooga a much larger, better-trained and more enthusiastic army than the one that had evacuated Corinth in late May. By the time they reached Chattanooga, they were plenty ready to go on the offensive.[27]

On the night of July 31, E. Kirby Smith traveled to Chattanooga to confer with Bragg and plan a daring counteroffensive. Bragg was unsure what his final destination would be, but prodding from the "Kentucky bloc," including Smith and John Hunt Morgan, forced Bragg's hand. Though Smith reported directly to the Confederate War Department, he offered Bragg false assurance that he would coordinate with Bragg and do as Bragg desired. In the end, Smith operated independently from Bragg, seeking the glory of liberation in Kentucky while Bragg was forced to lug his much larger army into the Bluegrass State a few weeks behind. Smith's nineteen thousand men of the Army of Kentucky were divided into four infantry divisions and one small cavalry brigade under Colonel John S. Scott. In staggered columns, Smith's men left Knoxville on August 12 and headed north toward Cumberland Gap. Because of Morgan's entrenched and well-supplied position there, Smith sent Patrick Cleburne's and Thomas Churchill's divisions through Rogers Gap, while ordering General Carter Stevenson's sizable division to make initial movements toward Cumberland Gap in order to occupy Morgan. Because Rogers Gap was so narrow, Smith ordered Henry Heth's division to carry the artillery and supply train through the wider Big Creek Gap. Once past Cumberland and Pine Mountains, Smith's divisions reconnoitered at Barbourville, with Stevenson staying behind to lock Morgan in place. Over the next several weeks, Smith would push north into the bluegrass of Kentucky, annihilating a Federal force under General Nelson at Richmond before marching into Lexington.

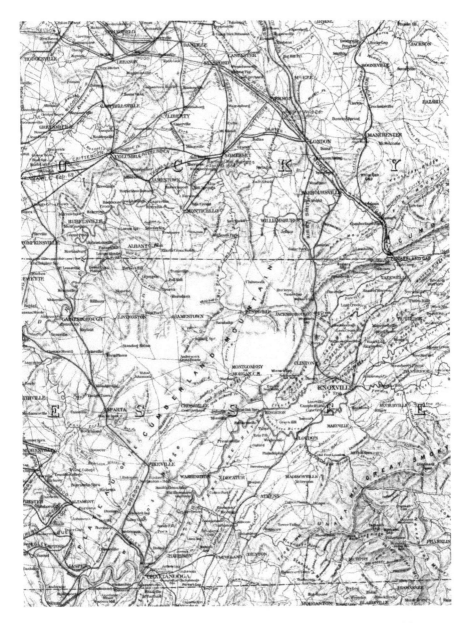

A map showing Bragg's and Smith's invasion paths into Kentucky. *Maps accompanying* OR.

George Morgan held out at Cumberland Gap as long as possible. Repeated forays along both sides of Cumberland Mountain, some led by Campbell Countians like Joseph Cooper and Lieutenant Colonel M.L. Philips intimately familiar with the terrain, nearly dislodged the Confederates.

Union general George Morgan exploded all of his ordnance in Cumberland Gap rather than leave it for the enemy when evacuating. This crater is evidence of the destruction.

Meanwhile, the heavily Cherokee Thomas Legion had joined the operations at Cumberland Gap, and some of their men scalped Federal soldiers killed at Baptist Gap just a few miles south of Cumberland Gap. By mid-September, Morgan realized that he was hopelessly surrounded and decided to evacuate

Cumberland Gap on September 17. Before leaving, Morgan destroyed the powder he had accumulated in a series of spectacular explosions. Craters from the explosion are still evident at Cumberland Gap today.[28]

Meanwhile, Bragg continued to organize his troops at Chattanooga, giving his men the necessary rest and recovery after the long slog from Mississippi. For Confederates on the plateau, these were the brightest moments of the war. Anticipating a great advance into Middle Tennessee and beyond, Private Moses Joseph Nichols of the Byrne neighborhood west of Cookeville in Putnam County reported on arriving in Chattanooga, "We feel like we have emerged from a land of despair to a land of felicity."[29] Angry at Federal troops "wickedly infesting our vicinities" and robbing "poor helpless women and children of their provisions" in Middle Tennessee, Nichols vowed to "liberate Tennessee." As for the armies of Buell and Mitchel operating on the west side of the plateau, the middling Putnam County farmer bragged to his family, "After we cut them off from their beef and crackers, they will fail to get backers and we will drive them off as a shepherd drives his herd, only we will be a little rougher than they usually are."[30]

Lafayette (Fayette) McDowell wrote in a similar spirit to his sister in Sparta: "We are all in good spirits now; the Yankee army is in about the same fix that ours was about the time we left Corinth."[31] Instead of men deserting as before, now more and more were joining. "Our men are now in the notion to fight." What changed Fayette's mind more than anything, however, was not the ebb and flow of military fortune; it was the impending emancipation policy heralded by the Second Confiscation Act, passed in July. "Since the late policy of the U.S. Government on slavery and the confiscation of property, there is no chance to compromise only by compelling to let us alone entirely," which, Fayette predicted, "they will be obliged to do."[32] A month before President Lincoln issued his preliminary Emancipation Proclamation in September, Confederate soldiers sensed that the Union army was about to launch the full-on assault against slavery that Confederates warned would happen in 1861. The electrifying effect of this shift in policy could be felt among Confederates of the Cumberland Plateau just as it could be among those from the Deep South.

On August 29, a day before Smith's victory at Richmond, Bragg and twenty-seven thousand troops organized into two corps under General Leonidas Polk and General William J. Hardee crossed the Tennessee River and began the march toward Bowling Green, Kentucky. It would involve the greatest movement of troops ever witnessed on the Cumberland Plateau and demonstrated a masterful usage of the terrain to shield his movements and stay on the move. The first movement was to climb Waldens Ridge on the Anderson Pike, which had been built by Josiah Anderson of northern Marion County. At the top of the plateau, Bragg's men turned left and descended into the Sequatchie Valley. Taking advantage of the straight roads and ready access to water in the Sequatchie, Bragg moved northeasterly, camping at Dunlap in Sequatchie County on the night of the thirtieth. At this point, Buell's Federals remained concentrated at Altamont in Grundy County with no idea of Bragg's plans. If Bragg were to head straight for Nashville, Altamont would be a good spot for Buell to observe him. If Bragg intended to go around Nashville and head for Kentucky, it would make better sense for Buell to occupy McMinnville or possibly Sparta to the north. None of Buell's plans mattered now. Bragg sent cavalry general Joe Wheeler to Altamont as a screening operation to confuse Buell of Bragg's intentions. Flummoxed by this action, Buell simply decided to retreat back toward Nashville and camp at Murfreesboro. He could at least protect the capital city while at Murfreesboro and turn north into Kentucky if Bragg bypassed him.[33]

Bragg continued up the Sequatchie Valley, turned left at Pikeville and ascended the plateau again. On top of the plateau, Bragg ventured through extremely rugged terrain in Van Buren County and the Cane Creek Gorge before crossing the Caney Fork River and entering the rolling hills of White County.[34] Bragg encamped at Sparta after the difficult trek over the Cumberland Plateau and plotted his next move. Darius Clark, a soldier with the Sixteenth Tennessee, Company G, from White County, recorded in his diary the difficult conditions of the march. After marching to Pikeville on September 1, his men rested for four hours before climbing the mountain in the rain. They then marched all night and "reached old Mr. Cranes at the foot of the mountain in Van Burain county" for a total of twenty miles. His spirits still up as he approached his home county, he recorded, "It is 11 miles from here to Sparta and the news is that we will go on to Cookville and on throw Kentucky."[35]

Bragg's men waited for days in Sparta for all the regiments to catch up before moving on. Arriving on the thirteenth, Fayette was finally able to visit his sister and share news of friends in the Twenty-fifth Regiment. But Fayette and Darius Clark continued north into Kentucky. Buell raced back to Louisville himself and fortified the city against an expected attack from Bragg. Instead, Bragg turned east to Bardstown, hoping to link up at long last with E. Kirby Smith. On October 4, Smith inaugurated Richard Hawes as the Confederate governor of Kentucky so he could enforce the Confederate draft. Federal troops on Frankfort's outskirts cut short the inaugural festivities. On October 8, thirsty men of Bragg's and Buell's army sought a common water source at Chaplin's Creek near Perryville. What followed was one of the bloodiest battles of the war. The result was mostly inconclusive, and Buell figured that Bragg would fight a second day. Instead, Bragg and Smith, finally together at Harrodsburg after the Battle of Perryville, turned around and headed back for the Cumberland Gap. They relished the piles of stores they obtained for their army. But the Kentucky Confederate dream was finished as Bragg ordered all Confederate forces out of Kentucky. He bemoaned the failure of Kentuckians to join the Confederate army, with only two thousand enlisting instead of the expected twenty thousand or more.[36]

Bragg and Smith returned to Tennessee through Cumberland Gap and continued to Knoxville and then to Chattanooga. At Chattanooga, the combined forces of Bragg and Smith moved northwest to Murfreesboro and were officially combined into the new Army of Tennessee. Bragg camped along the banks of Stones River, hoping to resupply his army from the rich countryside and block any potential Federal advance toward Chattanooga. At the same time, President Lincoln replaced Buell with William Starke Rosecrans after Buell's sluggish pursuit of Bragg following the Battle of Perryville. Rosecrans had earned plaudits at the Battles of Iuka and Corinth in September. Arriving in Nashville, he renamed his forces the Army of the Cumberland and provisioned the army for an offensive toward Chattanooga.[37] Rosecrans advanced toward Bragg's encampment on December 27, with a full battle taking place on New Year's Eve. After a day of respite, the battle resumed on January 2, and Rosecrans emerged victorious in what was the deadliest battle of the entire Civil War in terms of percentages of men engaged in the fighting.[38] The Battle of Stones River made Rosecrans a hero in the North at a time when the Union army suffered embarrassing defeats at Fredericksburg, Virginia, and Chickasaw Bayou, Mississippi. It also provided a military victory to support Lincoln's issuance of the Emancipation Proclamation. Within Tennessee, the Murfreesboro result forced Bragg to retreat southeastwardly to a more defensible position along the Duck River. Fighting would not resume on a large scale for six months, as both sides attempted to replenish their armies for a new year of campaigning.

Though Bragg and Smith had little luck recruiting for the Confederacy in Kentucky, they were able to increase their forces while in Tennessee thanks to conscription. Western plateau counties, never exempted from conscription, added many new companies of men, including those reorganized as the original twelve-month enlistments finished in May and June. Many young

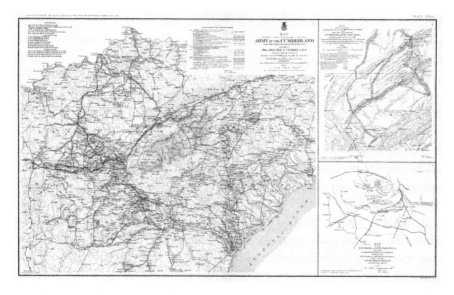

Union Army of the Cumberland map of operations. Note the Lower Cumberland Plateau in the center of operations in Tennessee.

men joined the Confederate army as it passed along the plateau in the summer of 1862. Henry Cagle of Sequatchie County, for example, enlisted in late August 1862, just as Bragg's men advanced through the neighborhood. It was in Sparta on September 5 that General Bragg issued Special Orders Number 1, initiating the draft across all of Tennessee. Bragg hoped that volunteers would fill the ranks, and he allowed men to volunteer in "such companies as they select," an important inducement to young men willing to follow their friends and kin into the army.[39]

Still, the Confederate cause was unpopular in East Tennessee. General Sam Jones, commanding East Tennessee from Knoxville after Smith's invasion of Kentucky, despaired of enforcing the conscription act. On September 21, he sought assistance from Governor Harris about how he should carry out the law's provisions.[40] One month later, with Bragg and Smith traveling through Knoxville, Jones begged Confederate secretary of war George Randolph to "suspend" the conscription act in East Tennessee due to continuing opposition.[41] Knoxville's Confederate congressman William G. Swan insisted, however, that conscription go forward as "the tories all through the country have it that the law will not be enforced," and if the law is suspended for "even one day," the effect will be to "embolden" the Unionists who may "resist outright."[42] Swan argued that the Confederate troops returning from Kentucky through East Tennessee were well placed to receive new conscripts into existing regiments, thereby limiting the effects on morale of putting the new soldiers into all-conscript regiments. But resentment against the draft was strong, even among staunch supporters of the Confederacy in East Tennessee. The *Chattanooga Daily Rebel*, a staunchly pro-Confederate newspaper, mocked Swan for supporting conscription in the Confederate Congress all the while refusing to enter the war himself. An editorial cited a recent case where Swan himself was accosted by conscription agents—described as "body snatchers"—at the Knoxville rail depot, to which Swan retorted that he was a congressman and should not be subject to the draft. Swan "would clench his fist and stamp his feet when he reflected on the disappointment to which he had been subjected at the depot, by the operation of that pet measure of his, the Conscript Act."[43]

With even pro-Confederate sources like the *Daily Rebel* expressing resentment against the draft, Unionists resisted by fleeing conscription agents and making their way into Kentucky. Counties to the west of the Lower Cumberland Plateau, including hotbeds of Confederate support like Lincoln County, also resisted the draft. In January 1863, as Bragg's men camped along the Duck River, General Gideon Pillow, head of the Board of Volunteer and Conscripts, prepared for a "conscript rake" to "clean out" Bedford County of able-bodied men, especially in the unusually pro-Union town of Shelbyville. As an extra appeal to the conservative Unionists of the region, Pillow invoked Lincoln's recently issued Emancipation Proclamation. The "tyrant and usurper, proposing to free all our slaves and taking them into his Army, and inciting the slaves to insurrection and massacre of their owners and their families, places him and his Government without the pale of civilization."[44] As Fayette McDowell commented to his sister, the fear of emancipation was a major rallying point for Confederates.

By late June 1863, replenished forces in the Union Army of the Cumberland had begun to move out of Murfreesboro toward Chattanooga. Bragg's reinforced Confederate Army of Tennessee stood ready to block Rosecrans's path along the Duck River at Tullahoma.[45] In a series of brilliant maneuvers around Liberty and Hoover's Gaps, Rosecrans advanced onto the Highland Rim and stood, once more, at the foot of the great Cumberland Plateau. Unlike Buell a year before, Rosecrans now benefited from a well-stocked supply line that could support advance operations along well-guarded railroads, rivers and turnpikes to Nashville and Louisville. Further evidence of impending doom for Confederate forces in East Tennessee came in the

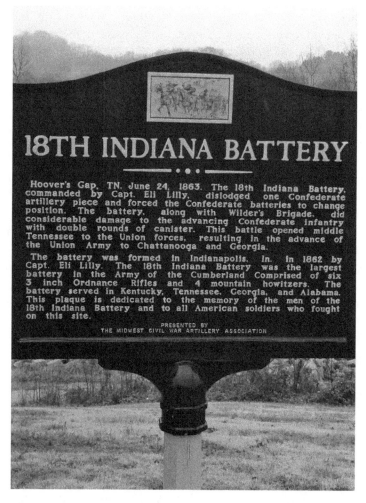

Captain Eli Lilly's Eighteenth Indiana Battery at Hoover's Gap on the Tullahoma campaign.

form of a dashing raid across the Cumberland Mountains, led by General William Sanders.[46] Flying down through Huntsville and Montgomery (Morgan County), Sanders raided supply depots from Kingston on to the east to Knoxville before returning to Kentucky. The effect was electrifying for Unionists, who finally dreamed of their own liberation. In early August, Rosecrans began to play the Cumberland Plateau hide-and-seek game that Bragg had done so effectively a year before. As Rosecrans's men first appeared on Stringers Ridge, Bragg noted that "mountains hide your foe from you, while they are full of gaps through which he can pounce on you at any time."[47] Confederate forces throughout East Tennessee nervously awaited the advancing Federal army.

Henry Campbell, traveling with the Eighteenth Indiana Battery from Tullahoma and over the Cumberland Plateau, kept a detailed journal where he recorded his observations of the beautiful, though barren, scenery. Climbing winding roads through rain and fog, Campbell reached a point above the clouds and took in "the grandest sight I ever witnessed."[48] On the remarkably flat mountaintop, Campbell camped at a place called University Springs, "spring of pure water right on top of the mtn," where "the state of Tenn intended to start a college here before the war." Campbell had reached Sewanee, the site of the future University of the South, where the misty scenery still enchants visitors today. Farther on, Campbell passed through Tracy City, mocked as a "city" with just three houses and a depot for the coal mine. Campbell was enchanted again as he reached the Sequatchie Valley, "one of the most beautiful and picturesque places that I ever had the fortune to gaze upon."[49] Reaching Stringer's Ridge just before Chattanooga, Campbell's men were greeted by Unionist civilians hiding from conscript officers, quoting one as saying, "We'uns [are] mighty glad to see you'uns."

Just a few days later, Bragg determined that his position at Chattanooga, and even at Knoxville, was no longer defensible. On September 1, Bragg ordered General Simon Bolivar Buckner to evacuate Knoxville. After brief siege operations on September 7, Burnside forced John W. Frazier to abandon Cumberland Gap once more. Bragg abandoned the great strategic prize of Chattanooga, as he no longer believed he could defend the city against Federal assaults from any of several invasion paths. Bragg retreated just south of Chattanooga to a camp along Chickamauga Creek, where he awaited General James Longstreet's reinforcements from the Army of Northern Virginia.[50]

The retreat worked remarkably well. After nearly trapping Rosecrans at McLemore's Cove, Bragg engaged in a massive battle against Rosecrans on September 19. After a day of horrific fighting, the carnage resumed on the second day. At a key moment in the battle, Rosecrans mistakenly plugged a gap in his lines that was not there. In the process, he created a real gap. At just the right time, General Longstreet's men arrived on the battlefield ready to pounce through the gap in Federal lines. The rout was on, as thousands of Federal soldiers ran to the north and west as fast as they could. Only the stout defense of Snodgrass Hill on the Federal left by General George Thomas prevented a historic catastrophe for the Union cause. Holding off Confederate attackers late in the afternoon, Thomas allowed the

Confederates controlled supplies coming into the besieged city of Chattanooga. Union supply routes required a sixty-mile journey until the cracker line was opened.

Army of the Cumberland to limp back into Chattanooga, defeated but still intact.[51] Bragg gingerly followed the Federals into Chattanooga but was in no shape to begin a major assault. Instead, he set up for a siege of Union forces in Chattanooga.

The last and greatest chapter of the Cumberland Plateau's Civil War military history now opened. Three ridges of the plateau would be especially critical in the ensuing siege and battle: Signal Mountain, Raccoon Mountain and Lookout Mountain. A fourth ridge, Missionary Ridge, was neither geologically nor geographically a part of the Cumberland Plateau. But its proximity to the plateau at Chattanooga made it a critical point for siege operations and for the eventual Federal escape. As Federal troops first limped into the city on September 21, Bragg placed his men atop Lookout Mountain and Missionary Ridge, where they held a commanding view of Union troops and their supply lines. Told that Union troops had less than a week's worth of rations, Bragg assumed that the demoralized Union troops would surrender shortly thereafter. A disillusioned William Rosecrans was removed from command of the Army of the Cumberland on September 29, to be replaced by George Thomas. William T. Sherman was ordered to move from Vicksburg with twenty thousand men. General Joseph Hooker, relieved of command just before the Battle of Gettysburg, was also ordered to Chattanooga. He would take fifteen thousand men in two corps on a lengthy rail voyage that rivaled Bragg's sojourn from Mississippi to Chattanooga in July.[52]

The supply situation was not as dire for Union troops as Bragg had supposed, as supplies were available for another month if managed properly. But the route into Chattanooga was treacherous enough. The Union army still held Bridgeport, Alabama, and the railroad from Nashville to that point. With Bragg on Lookout Mountain, Union forces could not bring supplies along the rail from Bridgeport into the city without facing certain destruction from sharpshooters. The only supply route from Bridgeport followed a wagon train into the Sequatchie Valley, up and over Waldens Ridge via the Anderson Turnpike and back down into Chattanooga from the north. Federal troops relayed signals to one another from atop Signal Mountain to communicate across the ridges of the plateau and into the Sequatchie Valley. Signalmen deployed coded messages notifying one another of coming supplies and impending danger. This mechanism was unwieldy and dangerous, however. And at sixty miles long, this Federal supply route was in danger of closure from the very beginning.[53]

On October 1, Bragg sent cavalry general Joseph Wheeler on a raid to shut down, or at least disrupt, this supply route. Wheeler's men intercepted wagons of supplies in the lower Sequatchie Valley and unleashed an orgy of destruction. Ordered to "kill the mules and burn the wagons," Wheeler's men plundered all they could, including barrels of whiskey. The latter may have done in Wheeler's raid in the end, as his increasingly drunken and disorderly men found less success raiding to the northwest past McMinnville. At Murfreesboro, Wheeler's raiders were forced to turn south and back into Alabama. They inflicted serious damage on Federal supplies and forced Federal troops in Chattanooga to live on "four cakes of hard bread and a quarter pound of pork" every three days by late October. Attempts to carry supplies along the banks of the Tennessee River by Browns Ferry were also futile, as Confederate sharpshooters lined the base of Raccoon Mountain and fired at will at hapless sutlers and mule drivers. The campaign had clearly reached a critical moment.[54]

For his part, Bragg faced a challenge to his leadership that turned out to be more acute than problems facing the Federal army. Blamed by much of the Confederate press for letting the Army of the Cumberland slip away from Chickamauga intact, Bragg sacked two of his subordinate commanders, Thomas Hindman and Leonidas Polk. Several other commanders then petitioned President Jefferson Davis to intervene and to remove Bragg from command over the Army of Tennessee. After an October 4 visit to the front lines, Davis reaffirmed Bragg's authority, allowing Bragg to sack further "trouble makers" like Simon Bolivar Buckner and D.H. Hill. The biggest remaining rival was James Longstreet. The two men would squabble over the next month, with serious consequences for the siege.[55]

General Ulysses Grant was ordered to appear in Chattanooga to help relieve Federal troops and open up a supply line. Arriving in mid-October, as the supply situation grew increasingly perilous, Grant and chief engineer William "Baldy" Smith began plans to seize Brown's Ferry across Moccasin Point and establish a straight "cracker line" from Chattanooga, down through Lookout Valley to Wauhatchie Station and west to Kelly's Ford, where the river was navigable to Bridgeport. The key would be to capture Browns Ferry, which Grant began to do on October 27. General William B. Hazen traveled the southerly route along the river from Chattanooga to Browns Ferry on a foggy night, out of sight of Confederate troops on Lookout Mountain. Fortunately for Grant, only two Alabama regiments guarded the river near Browns Ferry, and Federal forces easily repulsed them after taking the ferry. Meanwhile, General Hooker concluded his lengthy trail west and south from Pennsylvania and arrived at Bridgeport and Lookout Valley in time to link up with Hazen's men. The cracker line was open. Longstreet, having ignored the troubling news at Browns Ferry, ordered an attack on the Union position at Wauhatchie Station. The nighttime battle ended in a stalemate, and the Union cracker line remained open.[56]

Meanwhile, the feud between Longstreet and Bragg intensified. At last, Bragg made one of the strangest decisions of the war, sending Longstreet up toward Knoxville in hopes of recapturing the railroad town and reopening the Confederate supply line from Virginia. The move, approved by Davis, would also have the benefit of separating the feuding Confederate commanders from each other. Longstreet headed up toward Knoxville on November 5—just as the Union position was strengthening with the new supply line and the arrival of Sherman at Chattanooga.[57] Bragg had split his army at the worst possible time. He and Longstreet would both pay the price later that month.

With Sherman on the Union left, Thomas in the center and Hooker on the right, Grant first occupied Orchard Knob on November 23. Hooker followed with an assault up Lookout Mountain in the small but spectacular "Battle Above the Clouds" to take the crest of Lookout Mountain on November 24. On the morning of the twenty-fifth, Sherman crossed the Tennessee River in hopes of securing the north end of Missionary Ridge. But the complex

Browns Ferry, where Union troops established the cracker line and opened up supplies to Chattanooga.

geography of the region did him in; he failed to take the left-most point and was stopped in his tracks. At the same time, Hooker stalled at Chickamauga Creek, where retreating Confederates burned a bridge. That left the Army of the Cumberland in the center, under the command of George Thomas, to seize the rifle pits on the floor of the ridge. But the men, still angry over Chickamauga, pushed right up the ridge. Confederate positions on the geographic—but not military—crest of the ridge could not shoot down at the Union assailants. In a panic, the Confederates turned and fled back to Georgia, with Chattanooga and its surrounding ridges now in Union hands.[58]

Meanwhile, James Longstreet put in a siege of his own around Knoxville. Launching a full attack against the northwest bastion of Fort Sanders, Longstreet's men fell into an icy ditch and were unable to scale the fort walls. Union soldiers easily picked off Longstreet's battle-hardened troops in the ditch and routed the Confederates in twenty minutes.[59] News of Sherman's impending arrival on a relief mission convinced Longstreet to abandon his siege of Knoxville and retreat to the east. By April, Longstreet had returned to Virginia, leaving virtually the entire state of Tennessee in Union hands.

From Signal Mountain looking toward Chattanooga, Raccoon Mountain and Lookout Mountain.

The war was far from over in Tennessee. John Bell Hood would launch an ill-fated invasion of Middle Tennessee that would result in the cataclysmic Battles of Franklin and Nashville in late 1864. However, it was not a conventional war that would rage along the Cumberland Plateau after the Battles of Chattanooga and Knoxville. It was a guerrilla war, which began as early as 1861 and gained intensity as the conventional war consumed the state. And just as with the conventional war, the guerrilla war would engulf the Cumberland Plateau in more bloodshed, mayhem and destruction than anywhere else in the state.

War Among the People

Julia Marcum vowed to defend her family at all costs. Sixteen years old when the war broke out, the Scott County girl watched in horror as Confederates, known locally as "Bull Pups," searched for her father, Hiram C. Marcum. It was September 1861, a month after Governor Isham Harris secured reelection, and East Tennessee's Confederate authorities applied pressure against the many Tories in their midst. As Scott County was a banner Unionist county and Hiram a relatively prosperous leader of the Union cause, he was a marked man. On September 7, with dozens of Confederate troops camped just a mile away, a squad approached the Marcum house and inquired about the whereabouts of Julia's father. She delayed and resisted the Bull Pups long enough for her father to escape to the woods. Angry at this obstinate evasion, Confederates with the Eleventh Tennessee Infantry returned in the middle of the night, though this time with a heavy scent of whiskey on their breaths. One of them broke into the house and barked his intention to kill both Hiram and all the women of the house. The other soldiers stood guard outside and searched for Hiram. The intruder choked Julia's mother, Permealia, and then chased her eldest sister, Didama, up the stairs. Julia and another sister, Manerva, screamed and then grabbed axes and began to fend off the attacker. Manerva dropped her axe, but Julia kept striking away at the attacker, who thrust a bayonet through her head and gouged out an eye. At that moment, Hiram emerged from the yard and shot the soldier dead. Amazingly, Julia Marcum survived, and her father moved the family just over the border into Kentucky, where he joined the Union army. Julia Marcum would be remembered for decades as a hero, often posing for pictures with her trusty axe and telling her story. She also received a pension in 1885, the only woman to draw a pension "without the aid of a soldier."[1] Of course, Julia Marcum was very much a soldier on that fateful night, in defense of her family.

The incident at the Marcum house in September 1861 had all the markings of a people's war, where lines between civilians and soldiers blurred. More remarkable than the fact that a woman used physical force to defend her family was the timing of the event. September 7, 1861, was three weeks before the Travisville Affair supposedly introduced the Civil War to the Cumberland Plateau and the state of Tennessee. This brand of irregular war began early on the Cumberland Plateau and never relented. In many ways, the actions of local, loosely organized scouts, partisans and guerrillas would precipitate more formal military action in the region. The cycle of guerrilla insurgency and counterinsurgency destabilized the region and accelerated the breakdown in social order. Not until the very last days of the Civil War—and in many cases, long after the "real" war ended—did this irregular people's war truly end.

Guerrilla war has long consumed the imagination of Americans, especially given its legendary Revolutionary War heritage among Massachusetts Minutemen and followers of the South Carolina Swamp Fox Francis Marion. Its pedigree in the history of warfare includes the Chinese Taoist Sun Tzu, Spanish guerrillas resisting Napoleon (from which the term "guerrilla" entered the English language) and the writings of Prussian theorist Carl von Clausewitz, who understood war to be "politics by other means" and thus inseparable from the affairs of civilians. As historian Daniel Sutherland has remarked in his extensive treatment of the subject, guerrilla war served many purposes during the Civil War. Guerrillas obstructed Federal armies and prevented them from achieving their strategic objectives, destroyed vital supply lines and generally made occupation a dangerous and demoralizing act.[2] Guerrilla tactics took many forms, with its practitioners given many names like bushwhacker, partisan, scout, ranger, militia, Home Guard and others. And the organizational structure of guerrilla war varied considerably over time and place, with conventional authorities on both sides attempting to exploit this powerful weapon while trying desperately to control it.[3]

At times, guerrillas would act in support of larger conventional forces—in reconnaissance, supply destruction, scouting, shielding—and at other times, they would operate for entirely local purposes, such as revenge and control over local loyalties and resources. Some forces, especially cavalry soldiers, acted in a conventional military manner at times and as guerrillas at other times. Whatever the form and name, guerrillas used irregular tactics not employed on the traditional battlefield, and they formed primarily to defend the household, however broadly they defined it.[4] They were the chief practitioners of a war among the people.

While guerrilla warfare appeared all across the South, it emerged with special intensity on the Cumberland Plateau for a number of reasons specific to the region. First, the plateau occupied a space notable for its divided loyalties, though marked irregularly through communities. Overlapping social networks and loyalties in places like Fentress, White and Marion Counties made for a constant ground-level struggle for control. The proximity of neutral, and then Unionist, Kentucky added a dimension of discord, especially in the minds of Confederates in the Upper Cumberland. Second, the complex topography lent itself perfectly to hit-and-run guerrilla tactics. Guerrillas could escape to the vast forests, through deep gorges and hollows and into natural rock houses for protection. Many guerrilla leaders intimately knew the landscape and exploited it to their advantage. Third, with tens of thousands of troops crossing the Cumberland Plateau on numerous occasions, conventional military activity spawned legions of guerrilla units designed to either assist or resist the passing armies. This was also true for military action in the vicinity of, though not on, the plateau. Fourth, the powerful bonds of communal loyalty in this rural region gave special meaning to the defense of households, which were often defined along extended kinship networks. As the Julia Marcum incident shows, women were every bit as invested in the defense of the household as men. Even if not always wielding axes, women often served as the vital "supply line" for guerrillas as they operated in the neighborhood.[5] Complicating this, of course, was the fracturing of these kinship networks under the pressures of war. Trusted friends and family one day could become bitter enemies the next. This was especially true as the war dragged on and disaffected Confederates took the loyalty oath to the Union. And fifth, powerful local leaders kept the flame of resistance alive from the first to the last days of the war. Unusually ruthless and charismatic men like Champ Ferguson, Tinker Dave Beaty, John Hughs and Cal Brixey continually vowed revenge for prior attacks and maintained their organizational strength throughout the war.

The effect of guerrilla war on the Cumberland Plateau was pure destruction: households, the economy, political relations, infrastructure, private dwellings and the slave system would all unravel during the Cumberland Plateau's war among the people. This chapter will discuss the chronological development of guerrilla warfare, without pretending

A monument placed in Crossville in 2000 dedicated to soldiers from Cumberland County on both sides. The county was divided almost perfectly in half in the Civil War.

to cover every single incident. It will address who made up and led the guerrilla forces and how they were deployed. The chapter will conclude with a discussion of the social effect of the people's war.

Evidence of guerrilla-style violence appeared as early as the June 1861 referendum on secession. Amanda McDowell and Mary Catherine Sproul reported widespread violent intimidation of Unionists. Meanwhile, Unionists blasted the entire Confederate government as illegitimate, despite the June 8 election result. When Governor Harris refused to consider the petition for separate East Tennessee statehood, most Unionists began to consider armed insurrection as a legitimate mode of resistance. One reason large-scale insurrection did not appear right away was the lack of weapons available to Unionists so far removed from friendly territory. In fact, much of the early guerrilla activity along the Upper Cumberland in the summer and fall of 1861 concerned plans to smuggle weapons to East Tennessee Unionists or to transport East Tennessee Unionists through Confederate lines to Kentucky. Writing to Unionist senator Andrew Johnson from Travisville on July 9, a merchant named C.B. Ryan warned of the sudden appearance of some three hundred men who planned to require the citizens to swear an oath of loyalty to the "Jeff Davis Confederacy." The troops had not yet begun the Confederate oath-swearing process, but "just as soon as they do attempt it we are determined to defend ourselves the best we can."[6] For now, however, the men had "no arms except our Country rifles and shotguns which we intend using should they make any attempt to drive out union men of Fentress County."[7]

A few days later, George W. Keith, a merchant from Morgan County, reported that Confederate troops were moving through the county on the way to Scott and Fentress Counties, with many of them treating "unoffending" Union citizens violently. The Confederate troops removed the United States flag at Montgomery, though Keith proudly reports that his wife then grabbed the flag back from them. Startled by this act of resistance from a woman, a Confederate officer present taunted her with a Rebel flag, telling her that soon "they should all bow to it."[8]

On July 13, Dr. Jonathan D. Hale, a prominent New Hampshire–born physician in northern Fentress County and a vehement Unionist, wrote to Andrew Johnson from Cincinnati of his intention to raise a "Lincoln regiment" from Fentress County. Two days later, Samuel Bush wrote to Johnson from Louisville on Hale's behalf, requesting "Rifles of some sort" to repel "400 Middle Ten Troops" that had recently arrived in the county. "If they can't possibly get rifles they want the next best gun they can get—Such an one as will be suited to a Guerrilla warfare."[9] Bush offered to transport these guns from Louisville to Clinton County, Kentucky, "somewhere near the line from whence they can be easily obtained by the Fentress Co people."[10]

The troubles around Fentress County had all the makings of an incipient guerrilla war. Citizens trapped behind enemy lines vowed armed resistance and openly sought the delivery of arms. Men and women alike defied the Confederate authorities and blasted the Confederate government and flag as illegitimate. But what made the events so ominous was the presence of equally vehement Confederate support in the same neighborhood. Around Travisville and Pall Mall, where C.B. Ryan vowed to fight the "Jeff Davis Confederacy," Andrew McGinnis hosted a major Confederate recruitment camp on his property. Among those enlisting in the Confederate service there were Willis Scott Bledsoe and Champ Ferguson. When Confederate soldiers at Camp McGinnis raided a Union supply site across the border in Kentucky in late September, Champ's brother Jim was among the Unionists attacking the Travisville encampment. As everybody in the neighborhood understood, the Unionists were not just in Kentucky or even in other parts of

Fentress County. They could be found in the neighborhood. The Civil War quickly devolved into a communal war in northern Fentress County, and guerrilla tactics—raids, attacks against civilians, brutality—would define the conflict there for years to come.

For their part, Confederate citizens grew especially anxious when Generals Albert Sidney Johnston and Simon Bolivar Buckner sent the bulk of the Rebel troops at Camp McGinnis to Bowling Green, Kentucky. A letter to Governor Harris signed by twenty-one prominent Confederates in Fentress and Overton Counties demanded a regiment of infantry or company of cavalry to guard the likely Union invasion route from Clinton County, Kentucky. Reporting on the harassment of civilians in Travisville, the letter cited the "notorious Jim Ferguson," who killed James Saufley at Travisville and "whose ambition seems to be to shoot Southern men in cold blood whenever he sees them." The Union raiders, aided by Union sympathizers within the neighborhood, marked "our best men" on the "black list of renegades" and stole "large portions of our grain, our hogs and beef-cattle, fine horses and mules, wagons, etc."[11] General Buckner insisted that the fears were misplaced and that not all Confederate troops had been removed to Bowling Green. Rather, Colonel Murray would remain on guard along the border, and Colonel Stanton would assist Murray's regiment however necessary to "break up the various Lincoln rendezvous" in southern Kentucky.[12]

It is important to keep in mind who composed the Confederate regiments then guarding the border. Colonel Sidney Smith Stanton of Jackson County commanded the Twenty-fifth Tennessee Infantry, which included regiments from White, Overton, Jackson and Putnam Counties—all in the Upper Cumberland. John M. Hughs, a future colonel in the regiment and a feared guerrilla leader, had been a hotelkeeper from Livingston and was elected a lieutenant in Company D in the Twenty-fifth. Colonel John P. Murray's Twenty-eighth Tennessee Infantry was also an Upper Cumberland unit. Originally known as the Second Tennessee Mountain Volunteers, the Twenty-eighth included men from Cumberland, Jackson, Overton, Putnam, Smith and White Counties. Murray had been one of Putnam County's secession leaders and helped prepare the county's secession resolutions in April.[13] Considering that the regiments guarding the border were made of the "best men" of the community, it makes sense that leading citizens would demand the regiments be kept in place. The ties between these regiments and the community would persist despite later consolidations and reorganizations, as leaders within the regiments would return home to form guerrilla bands that, in their minds, continued to defend their communities as before.

Along the border, it was clear that an eruption of large-scale Unionist guerrilla activity was imminent. The only question is whether the event really counts as "guerrilla war" at all. On November 8, conspirators burned five bridges along the East Tennessee and Virginia and East Tennessee and Georgia Railroads in hopes of cutting off Confederate communications between Richmond and Tennessee and fomenting a large-scale Unionist rebellion. General Sherman's last-minute refusal to send troops into Tennessee through the Clinton-Fentress County border area left the saboteurs vulnerable to arrest. The resulting crackdown pressured hundreds of Union men to flee through Confederate lines to Kentucky and enlist in Union regiments. But was this really a form of guerrilla warfare? Sabotage against infrastructure is a standard part of conventional war and was deployed on both sides on numerous occasions. What gave the incident its guerrilla character was not the conspiracy behind it but the reliance on civilians in civilian clothing, who otherwise gave no indication of their military activity. They were never enrolled in the Union army as soldiers, and they did not wear Union uniforms. As Governor Harris, Colonel Danville Ledbetter and President Jefferson Davis understood, these partisan fighters could be found anywhere in East Tennessee. It would take a more vigorous counterinsurgent campaign to stifle them and prevent any shipments of arms to them, all the while defending against conventional military invasion from Kentucky.

The tide changed dramatically in the Upper Cumberland with the New Year. Confederate defeat at Mill Springs in January 1862 and the chaotic retreat along the Cumberland River into Tennessee brought the full force of guerrilla war back to the Upper Cumberland after a brief hiatus. It was during this chaotic moment of retreat that some of the most renowned figures in the Upper Cumberland's guerrilla war first announced their presence. This was especially true of Tinker Dave Beaty, a Unionist who organized his Independent Scouts in the East Fork of the Obey River in February 1862. After the war's conclusion, Beaty testified in the trial against Champ Ferguson and explained how he had begun his career as a Unionist guerrilla. It was "10 or 12 days after the Mill Springs fight…several of Bledsoe's men came to my house and told my wife to tell me I must take sides in the war or leave the country." Returning from the field with his two sons and a neighbor, Beaty fired on the men. This would turn out to be the first of many encounters, as "they kept running in on us every few weeks, Ferguson, Bledsoe and others, killing and driving people off." Beaty vowed to defend his home; "if they killed me, let them kill me."[14]

Dr. Jonathan Hale and Tinker Dave Beaty, two militant Unionists from the Upper Cumberland.

Beaty exemplified the guerrilla ethic. He fought in defense of his household and community, and he eschewed all regular military protocol in his lengthy struggle with rival Confederate bands. His men were mustered into the Union army on January 25, 1862—just after Mill Springs—though he was never paid for his service. A review of the personnel in David Beaty's Independent Scouts reveals a tightly connected web of neighbors and kin from the valley of the East Fork of the Obey River. Certain surnames repeat with regularity—Beaty,

Choate, Bowles (sometimes spelled Boles), Smith and Winningham. The map of farms in the East Fork shows the geographic proximity of the Beaty men to one another. Census returns for the neighborhood reveal a community with few class divisions and virtually no slaves. It would be an exaggeration to say that Beaty's men lived in isolation from the outside world; the Boatland community had long been linked to the rest of the Upper Cumberland area by logging and stock trading. But relative to the merchants at Jamestown or Livingston who composed the bulk of Confederate leadership or the wealthier McGinnises in the fertile Wolf River Valley at Pall

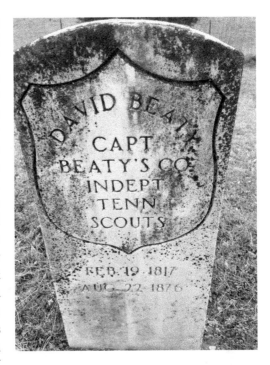

The gravestone of Tinker Dave Beaty in the Beaty-Lacy Cemetery near the East Fork of the Obey River.

Mall, the Beaty neighborhood was comparatively closed. Leadership in the East Fork was defined not by access to wealth, power and prestige in the wider world but by kinship, age and tradition. Alas, Tinker Dave was not only kin to many of the scouts in his command. He was also, at forty-four years of age in 1861, the oldest among them.

At the same time Beaty organized his Independent Scouts, a Home Guard in Scott County began to take action against Confederate troops. The guard was formed as early as December 28, 1861, when organizers at the courthouse in Huntsville swore an oath that read:

We the undersigned agree and pledge ourselves to each other in a covenant and by our oaths to unite together in a company by the name of a home guard to protect our homes, families, property, and liberties and our neighbors and their property and liberties and also to protect the constitution and the union…and we also bind ourselves to keep a profound secret of all matters concerning our meeting places and the times of our meetings, and what may be done by us, or any of our people in defense of our Rights, and if any of us shall prove to be a traitor or do any thing that may conflict with this obligation he shall be dealt with at the discretion of our Captain.[15]

The signatories to this oath included a cross-section of Scott County's population, joined by a handful of men who had lived in Fentress County as recently as 1860. As Scott County historian Paul Roy notes, Confederate authorities treated these men as "bushwhackers" who became "marked men."[16] What Julia Marcum's family experienced in September was likely the fate of these Home Guards and their families if they were not careful. Many of these Home Guards also served as pilots for Unionists from elsewhere in East Tennessee seeking safety in Kentucky.[17]

In Morgan County, a Home Guard company led by Captain Duncan was more active. In early February 1862, Colonel Ledbetter sent the First Tennessee Cavalry to Camp Schuyler near Wartburg and found himself in a pitched battle with "the traitors of Scott and Morgan counties," with Captain Duncan among the dead.[18] Lieutenant Colonel J.W. White of the First Tennessee Cavalry (CSA) reported as many as three hundred "Lincolnites," who fought a "running battle" for over an hour. The Union guards were "on a mountainside and deemed themselves inaccessible."[19] Considering the sculpted gorges and mazes of boulder gardens in the landscape of Morgan and Scott Counties, it is easy to imagine how the guerrilla fighters could make themselves "inaccessible." Later, irregular cavalry leadership in Morgan County from former sheriff Meshack Stephens affirmed the legitimacy of the Union cause in the county.[20]

Ledbetter feared a Union invasion again and desperately worked to plug the gaps along Cumberland Mountain. He continued to hunt Unionist guerrillas in Morgan, Scott and Campbell Counties, facing continual "small parties from inaccessible points."[21] Ledbetter had reason to worry. Though the Union army was committed mostly to a Middle and West Tennessee invasion strategy, official organization of Unionist cavalry units on both sides of the Tennessee-Kentucky border continued apace. Most important was the work of William Clift, a millionaire land speculator and gristmill operator from Soddy in Hamilton County. Described by one contemporary as "the most ultra of the ultraists of East Tennessee,"[22] Clift assembled the Seventh Tennessee Infantry Regiment, with Huntsville and Scott County as its main base of operations.[23] Though formally organized through the Federal army, the Seventh Tennessee Infantry was essentially a guerrilla or partisan unit, tasked with "harassing the enemy's rear" on

Cumberland Mountain and weakening the Confederate occupation generally.[24]

Clift's force was strong enough by the summer of 1862 to attract significant Confederate attention. Clift regularly raided Morgan and Anderson Counties—always at "the request of our Union friends"—to capture Confederate guards or destroy Confederate property. By August 13, as E. Kirby Smith began preparations for his invasion of Kentucky, the Confederate general reached his wits' end with Clift's guerrillas. Smith sent roughly nine hundred soldiers to Clift's "eminence" near Huntsville and routed the poorly trained men in the so-called Battle of Huntsville.[25] Clift insisted in his report that some of

Colonel William Clift, an "ultra" Unionist from Sale Creek in Hamilton County who organized the Seventh Tennessee Infantry (USA). *Courtesy of Chattanooga Public Library.*

the Home Guard leaders, like William Robbins and William Shelton, had fought "with coolness and deliberation."[26] Indeed, Confederate authorities in Knoxville remained wary of Clift, especially as the bulk of Smith's men were in Kentucky. Clift's men were suspected of "awaiting an opportunity to attack some vulnerable point—probably Loudon."[27]

Smith had good reason to worry, as Clift resumed his activities once the Confederates returned to Tennessee in October. But by this point, his target was not the conventional forces in command from Knoxville; rather, it was a gang of Confederate guerrillas that had become the most significant threat to the safety of Union-supporting civilians in the Upper Cumberland. As Clift wrote in late October, "I deem it highly indispensable to break up these guerrilla companies as speedily as possible." The fiercest guerrilla company that had ranged east and west between Overton and Scott Counties, and into Wayne and Clinton Counties Kentucky, was led by Champ Ferguson.

No guerrilla in Tennessee or Kentucky captured more attention, then or now, than Champ Ferguson. One of the few men tried, convicted and hanged for war crimes, Ferguson's postwar trial produced a detailed record of his guerrilla career. Ferguson was convicted of fifty-three murders, though he bragged that he killed twice as many. As the study of guerrilla conflict has become a mature subfield in the historiography of the Civil War, Champ Ferguson has been reassessed by recent scholars, with the work of historian Brian McKnight standing above the rest. McKnight explains the sociopathic logic and psychological dualism of Ferguson clearly: every man Champ killed, he did so because he had reason to believe his victim would have killed him first. Born and raised in Clinton County, Kentucky, Champ Ferguson found himself in legal trouble in 1859 after killing a Fentress County constable trying to arrest him for illegally "recovering" his livestock. Champ's attorney in Jamestown was the well-respected Willis Scott Bledsoe, who later "convinced" Champ that if the Confederacy were to win the coming Civil War, all charges against Champ would be dropped. However specious the reasoning, it was enough to convince Champ Ferguson to defy his own family and join the Confederate army.

In many ways, Champ Ferguson was unique among guerrillas. First, whereas many Confederate guerrillas took to the bush after serving a year in conventional military service, Champ's violent guerrilla career began almost immediately with the outbreak of war along the Kentucky-Tennessee border. In August 1861, Champ was arrested by Unionist Home Guards in his native Clinton County, suspected of Confederate loyalty because of his noted presence around Camp McGinnis. While he was taken as a prisoner en route to Camp Dick Robinson, Champ escaped and headed back into Tennessee. As McKnight notes, "His arrest and forced march toward Camp Dick Robinson made a profound impression on Ferguson."[28] The refrain "Did you go to Camp Robinson?" would be his murderous calling card before shooting and stabbing many of his victims. Ferguson joined the cavalry unit organized by his attorney, Scott Bledsoe, and participated in several cross-border skirmishes over the next several months. But Ferguson did more than raid supplies and attack Home Guard and Union encampments. He developed a hit list in his mind of men who were responsible for his arrest and who might threaten further violence against him. This began with the shooting of William Frogge in his sickbed on November 1, 1861, and followed with the murder of Champ's longtime friend, but now "Lincolnite" enemy, Reuben Wood. Demanding of Wood, "Don't you beg, and don't you dodge," Ferguson shot Wood in front of his family, just as he had killed

Frogge.[29] Ferguson was not the first guerrilla in the Upper Cumberland, but he was likely the first to execute every foe who came within sight.

Second, though most guerrillas imagined themselves to be a conservative force defending the social network to which they belonged, Champ violently severed ties with his Clinton County kin. Champ developed a new network of followers and admirers based, in part, on his record of ruthlessness. His own brothers, Jim and Ben, were militant Unionists, with Jim carrying a reputation as violent as Champ's. Indeed, Clinton County was one of the most Unionist counties in Kentucky, and Champ's embrace of the Rebel cause made him a truly hated man in his community. Completely breaking ties with his county of birth, he moved south to White County in the spring of 1862 and made his home for the rest of the war on a farm near the Calfkiller River.

Third, the brutality of Champ's violence seemed to predate the more sordid acts of violence committed by others on the Cumberland Plateau. By 1864, dozens of guerrillas were mutilating their victims' bodies, torturing their prisoners or taking special delight in killing wounded men in front of sobbing and begging wives and children. But in late 1861 and early 1862, Champ was one of the few men to employ such vicious tactics. Champ Ferguson typically stabbed his victims in the heart after they had been shot—though likely to ensure the victim had died rather than out of any grotesque pleasure in the act. Willing to murder men in their homes in front of their families, Champ's tactics breached the distinction between criminal civilian and military violence.

Finally, Champ Ferguson melded the personal and the political more fully than any other guerrilla. Especially in the early part of the war, Champ would often kill his victims simply for the crime of having "gone to Camp Dick Robinson." In Champ Ferguson's eyes, any Tennessean or Kentuckian who went to Camp Dick Robinson would be joining the Union army and, consequently, threaten Champ's life. The world had been divided into those who meant to kill him and those who did not. In what he later described as a "miscellaneous war" along the border, "every man was in danger of his life: if I hadn't kill[ed] my neighbor, he would have killed me. Each of us had from 20 to 30 proscribed enemies, and it was regarded as legitimate to kill them at any time, at any place, under any circumstances."[30] Of course, much of Champ's "defensive" violence was preemptive in nature. With thousands of Kentuckians and Tennesseans having "gone to Camp Robinson" at some point, Champ's target list was practically endless.

What is most interesting here is how Champ Ferguson fits within the larger context of guerrilla warfare on the Cumberland Plateau.

The grave of Champ Ferguson in the France Cemetery, north of Sparta. The comb grave style is common in the Upper Cumberland.

Matters of place and time are critical for understanding Champ Ferguson's relationship to other guerrillas on both sides. First is the matter of state loyalty. Not only was Kentucky a Union state after September 1861, but Clinton County was also a banner Union county. And while many of the Confederates in nearby Fentress and Overton Counties were reluctant to secede, they quickly developed a border war mentality that emphasized "take no prisoners" fighting. Even without Champ Ferguson, large-scale guerrilla violence would almost certainly have developed along the lawless No Man's Land of the Upper Cumberland. Though he began his own vicious guerrilla career earlier than most, Champ became an uncontrollable menace to Unionist civilians when others joined him from the bush. Also critical was the presence—or lack thereof—of conventional military forces to protect the Confederate-leaning citizenry against potential attack. Most of the other guerrillas joined Champ Ferguson when the conventional forces tasked with protecting the Confederate citizens of the Upper Cumberland, notably the Twenty-fifth and Twenty-eighth Tennessee Infantry and the Fourth Tennessee Cavalry Regiments, moved away from the region.

After Mill Springs, Fort Donelson and the fall of Nashville in late February 1862, the Union army sought control over as much of Middle Tennessee as it could hold. The Upper Cumberland would fall right along the dividing line between land still under Confederate control out of Knoxville and the outer reaches of Union general Don Carlos Buell's Army of the Ohio in Nashville. In March 1862, guerrillas from both sides tried to calm things down after an orgy of violence following the Confederate retreat from Mill Springs. Meeting at Monroe, near the Confederate Camp of Instruction at Camp Myers, representatives from Overton, Fentress and Clinton Counties hammered out an agreement to refrain from raiding in one another's home counties. Present on the Union side were Tinker Dave Beaty and his two sons, James and Claiborne, and several Kentucky Unionists; the Confederate side included Livingston lawyer Winburn Goodpasture, Monroe merchant Landon Armstrong, a very wealthy farmer named Jessie Roberts and Champ Ferguson.[31] Other than Champ and Tinker Dave's sons, most of these representatives were older men respected in their communities.[32] It turned out to be a last and futile attempt to stop the bloodshed, as Confederate raids in Clinton County resumed within days of the supposed peace arrangement. Instead of reaching peace, Confederate and Unionist guerrilla activity increased in volume and intensity as the power vacuum widened in the Upper Cumberland.

In addition to the Bledsoe-Ferguson band were two other major independent guerrilla forces that began to operate in the wake of Mill Springs. One unit, led by the Livingston attorney James McHenry, raided the border counties of Kentucky in the spring of 1862. Another outfit, led by Jackson County farmer Oliver Perry Hamilton, targeted Unionists along the Lower Wolf River Valley. Hamilton's brutality and motives nearly matched those of Ferguson, including "finishing off" a wounded young victim while in his mother's arms.[33] In Hamilton's crosshairs was Dr. Jonathan D. Hale, the New Hampshire–born Unionist who requested arms from Andrew Johnson for Unionists in East Tennessee and the Upper Cumberland. Hamilton arrested Hale and threatened to kill him but then released him into Kentucky for reasons unknown. Hamilton and Ferguson would become close associates as the war progressed. It was in retaliation for the death of Hamilton while in Union captivity in 1864 that Ferguson justified his most infamous killing of all: the murder of Lieutenant Elza Smith near Saltville, Virginia. In October 1864, Ferguson, with his sidekick Raine Philpott, accused Smith of executing Hamilton and paid the wounded Smith a deathly visit while he was in the Emory hospital.

Several developments in the spring and summer of 1862 intensified the guerrilla war: passage of the Confederate Partisan Ranger Act in April 1862, the conclusion of twelve-month Confederate enlistments in May, Bragg and Smith's invasion of Kentucky in August and September and the intensification of Confederate conscription in September. Each of these actions applied wartime pressure on ordinary civilians and forced men and women alike to pick sides and commit to a cause. The Partisan Ranger Act, which gave formal authority to independently operating regiments, was passed as Confederate forces were on the defensive in both eastern and western theaters. Confederate political and civilian leaders expressed mixed opinions on the act and on the value of guerrilla war in general. Robert E. Lee and Jefferson Davis loathed the undisciplined and demoralizing nature of irregular combat, while others viewed it as the best chance to undermine Federal occupation. Importantly, passage of the Partisan Ranger Act was followed closely by the termination of original twelve-month enlistments for men in the Army of Tennessee. As a result, the Confederate Army of Tennessee thoroughly reorganized itself after the loss of Corinth in late April, with many junior officers seizing the opportunity to return home to organize either partisan ranger units or new cavalry commands. Among those would be Hamilton, Bledsoe and White County's George Dibrell.

John Hunt Morgan's first raid into Kentucky in June 1862 incorporated many of the independent guerrilla companies, including that of Champ Ferguson. Morgan exemplified both the guerrilla and Southern cavalryman ideal—he was brave, dashing, reckless and ruthless.[34] Meanwhile, John P. Murray, former colonel of the Twenty-fifth Infantry, organized the Fourth Tennessee Cavalry Regiment, which served as a kind of organizational superstructure for many guerrilla outfits on the Cumberland Plateau. Included in Murray's Fourth were companies belonging to McHenry, Bledsoe, Ephraim Hixson and Oliver Schoolfield of Bledsoe County; M.A. Christian of Putnam County; and George W. Carter of Van Buren County. This regiment was thoroughly reorganized on multiple occasions such that the company commanders were known more popularly. Hamilton, more in the vein of the independent Champ

Ferguson, formed an official Partisan Ranger unit called Hamilton's Cavalry Battalion in December 1862. Only Hughs, now promoted to colonel, remained in the Twenty-fifth Infantry. In August 1863, Bragg issued Order No. 217, which authorized Hughs to return home and round up absentees and deserters.[35] Bragg also sent Captain J.J. Ammonet and his cavalry company to join Hughs in what turned out to be a major guerrilla campaign in White County.[36]

Beginning especially in 1863, as the Confederate army retreated toward Chattanooga from Murfreesboro, guerrilla warfare changed character in some important ways. First, as more semi-official Confederate companies engaged in guerrilla activities, the Federal army applied more vigorous counterinsurgency measures. Second, as the bulk of the fighting drifted toward Chattanooga, the center of guerrilla war shifted toward White County, the Sequatchie Valley and the mountains around Chattanooga. Confederate guerrilla commanders like George Dibrell and George W. Carter, based in the central and southern plateau, became more active in the guerrilla struggle. Taking the initiative on the Federal side were cavalry commanders William B. Stokes and James P. Brownlow and Union guerrillas like Rufus Dowdy and Calvin Brixey. Third, a new element entered the fray: Confederate desertion. To counter the alarming rates of desertion as the Army of Tennessee retreated in Georgia, Bragg sent several junior officers to round up new enlistees. Many of these officers would join forces with Confederate guerrilla bands. At the same time, the Union cavalry scooped up hundreds of these deserters willing to take an oath of loyalty to the United States. From these were formed some of the more colorful and controversial Union regiments of the war. And finally, the cumulative effect of guerrilla war along the plateau meant the complete collapse in law and order, with banditry rampant and economic activity virtually ceasing.

General Rosecrans began to address seriously the Confederate guerrilla threat in the Upper Cumberland in February 1863. But his intention was mostly to secure a supply line up the Cumberland River so that the army would not have to rely on railroads vulnerable to the disruptions of John Hunt Morgan, Joe Wheeler and Nathan Bedford Forrest. Rosecrans sent cavalry forces to the east from Murfreesboro toward Liberty in DeKalb County.[37] For this mission, Rosecrans turned to the former congressman from Liberty, William B. Stokes, to lead his Fifth Tennessee Cavalry into the area. Stokes had come under fire for disciplinary problems in his unit, and his men would be criticized much more over the next year. But he was arguably the best man for counterinsurgent operations in his old home turf, as he could

Colonel William B. Stokes of DeKalb County commanded the Fifth
Tennessee Cavalry (USA), which took on John Hughs's Confederate
guerrillas in 1863 and 1864. *Courtesy of United States Library of Congress.*

round up supporters and scouts to take the fight to Confederate guerrillas
still controlling the Caney Fork Valley.

On the fifteenth, Rosecrans ordered navy lieutenant LeRoy Fitch to patrol
the Cumberland River as far as Carthage and destroy any Confederate
gunboats under construction either there or farther up the Caney Fork
River.[38] He was especially worried about John Hunt Morgan, who was then
assembling men for the purposes of crossing the Cumberland and invading
Kentucky. But Fitch and cavalry general George Crook discovered a different
kind of trouble beyond Carthage: "rebel hordes of cavalry...conscripting
and carrying off provisions."[39] Crook and Fitch hoped to extend the supply
line up to Celina and then down the Wolf and Obey River into Overton and

Fentress County. But Confederate guerrillas continued to pick off their easy prey.[40] On March 21, Crook wrote to General James Garfield a desperate letter detailing guerrilla attacks on his supply stores and concluded, almost as a non sequitur, with a question: "Who is 'Tinker Dave' Beatty?"[41] It would take many months for the Federal army to figure out how to exploit this valuable Union guerrilla in the Upper Cumberland, but it was becoming apparent that Confederate guerrillas themselves were posing a problem that needed to be addressed if Rosecrans was going to have any success pushing toward Tullahoma and Chattanooga.

Meanwhile, Confederate guerrillas spent much of their time searching for able-bodied young men to press into service. The search for conscripts and deserters led to one of the most heartbreaking tragedies of the Cumberland Plateau's Civil War. At some point in May 1863, Confederate guerrillas surrounded the cabin of the Tackett family along Charit and Station Camp Creek near the Big South Fork in Scott County. A woman inside the cabin desperately tried to hide her two teenaged grandsons targeted by the guerrillas. She told them to crawl into the little space underneath a feather mattress and down quilt on her bed. When the guerrillas arrived, she claimed she was too sick to move from atop the bed, so the guerrillas did not search under her bed. After a long and fruitless search for the Tackett boys, the guerrillas left. The woman then removed her mattress and found, to her horror, that the two boys had suffocated in their hiding place. She buried the two boys in a makeshift grave outside the cabin, simply marked "MA 1863"; the National Park Service at Big South Fork has preserved the grave site and remains of the Tackett homeplace. Tragic stories like these rarely made their way into official military records. But they were common experiences nonetheless that residents along the Cumberland Plateau passed down through oral tradition to their descendants.[42]

With the Union army heading toward White County in late July, Amanda McDowell commented on the experience of being surrounded by guerrillas and counter-guerrillas. Hearing of Unionist bushwhackers, McDowell commented, "The Yankees are getting close…From all I can learn it is a part of Stokes' rgt who have got in there by some means and are after the Southern soldiers, &c…and they do as the Southern soldiers do a great many times, take revenge on those who happen to be of the opposite party."[43] She then offered a fitting assessment of the guerrilla war as a whole: "The truth is, each side, when it gets a little the advantage and gets of the opposite party trodden down a little, crows a little too big, and when the trodden party gets a chance to, retaliates rather severely."[44]

On August 8, Colonel Robert H.G. Minty of the Fourth Michigan led a full-on attack of troops under the command of George Dibrell around Sparta. Leaving McMinnville and passing through Spencer in Van Buren County, Minty crossed the Caney Fork and attacked Dibrell's men in the Hickory Valley, south of Sparta, and then reached Camp Leftwich north of town. Dibrell's men retreated to his own nearby farm, where the two sides continued to skirmish along the junction of Wild Cat Creek and the Calfkiller River. Champ Ferguson and other "citizens" reinforced Dibrell in the fight, and Minty retreated back to the Caney Fork.[45] The battle was inconclusive but would be resumed again a week later. This time, Minty

Top: The fireplace of the Tackett homeplace near Charit and Station Camp Creek in Big South Fork National River and Recreation Area.

Left: The grave of one of the teenaged boys who suffocated under their grandmother's mattress while hiding from Confederate guerrillas.

came through Sparta with a larger cavalry force and was guided through the difficult terrain by one of Dibrell's own slaves. Fighting erupted at Yankeetown, north of Sparta. This time, it was Dibrell's men who fled after the battle, heading east at night over the Cumberland Plateau and down to Kingston. Amanda McDowell reported that "the Yankees have rather made a scatterment of Dibrell's men," though Dibrell himself described his movement as a strategic withdrawal of his smaller force to a high point to avoid flanking.[46] Either way, Dibrell was gone, Minty moved south toward Pikeville and Chattanooga and the residents of Sparta found food harder and harder to obtain in the wake of multiple cavalry engagements and guerrilla raids.

One of the biggest changes in fortune for the people of the Cumberland Plateau came with the Federal invasion of East Tennessee on September 1. As Bragg ordered a strategic withdrawal of all his forces out of Knoxville and Chattanooga, Ambrose Burnside's Army of the Ohio followed multiple routes over the plateau into Knoxville. Though it made strategic sense for Bragg to reconnoiter in North Georgia, it demoralized many Tennessee Confederates and fueled more and more desertions. With Confederate guerrillas in the Upper Cumberland now surrounded by Federal troops to the east and west, the fighting became increasingly desperate. Burnside began to organize and arm his own Home Guards in the Cumberland and Great Smoky Mountains. And he ordered Tinker Dave Beaty to "go to the mountain forks and the Rebels and keep the roads open in exchange for all the ammunition he and his men needed."[47]

But Sparta would be a difficult prize to hold, especially as it had become the prime rendezvous for Confederate guerrillas from all parts of the Cumberland Plateau in 1863. North and east of the Caney Fork, south of the Cumberland River and west of the Cumberland Plateau lay the ultimate No Man's Land that would witness a "perfect reign of terror" between September 1863 and May 1864. James P. Brownlow entered the scene in late November with his First Tennessee Cavalry, and he established a new policy: "I would take no prisoners."[48] McDowell reported, "The whole country is in an uproar. The news is that the Yankees killed some of their prisoners after they had surrendered. The Yanks say that Southern soldiers did so, so we hear."[49]

Over the next five months, White County would remain a killing field, with several brutal guerrilla engagements and counterinsurgent operations along the Calfkiller River. Hughs took command of all guerrilla forces, while Brownlow and Stokes led Federal forces from Sparta. The most violent episode happened on February 22, when Stokes's men walked into a perfect ambush along the Calfkiller at Dug Hill. Knowing that Brownlow and Stokes would take no prisoners, Hughs's collection of guerrillas "never fought with more desperation or gallantry" than on that day.[50] After the Federals under Captain Exum were wounded in the initial volley, Confederate guerrillas bashed in the heads of some of the captives with rocks, slit the throats of other men and finished off the remainder with single shots to the head.[51] Making matters worse as far as Stokes was concerned, some of the Confederates were wearing blue uniforms.[52] Stokes complained in his report, "Deserters from the rebel army are constantly joining Hughs. The people are thoroughly and decidedly disloyal…The country is rocky and mountainous, and very bad for cavalry…I have to fight rebel soldiers and citizens, the former carrying the arms and doing the open fighting; the latter, carrying news and ambushing."[53]

After the so-called Calfkiller Massacre, Federal troops concentrated at Sparta with the intention of annihilating the guerrilla bands once and for all. The effect was mostly to squeeze the guerrillas to the south. On March 18, Stokes surprised and raided Hughs and Bledsoe near Beersheba Springs in Grundy County and generally scattered Hughs from the region.[54] Adding to the mix in Grundy County was a new unit called the First Alabama and Tennessee Vidette Cavalry, composed mostly of deserters from the Confederate army and feared deserter turned Unionist guerrilla Calvin Brixey. This unit was every bit as notorious among Southern sympathizers in the Lower Cumberland as Champ Ferguson's band was in the Upper Cumberland. Brixey joined the Sixteenth Tennessee Infantry (CSA) in July 1861 along with many others from the barrens of Warren, Coffee, Grundy and Franklin Counties. He deserted after the loss at Corinth and began his own bushwhacking career shortly afterward. When the Vidette Cavalry was organized in the summer of 1863, Brixey joined and eventually became captain of Company D. His men included poorer men from Grundy County who resented their wealthier neighbors who had led the secession drive in the spring of 1861.[55] After murdering dozens of men, Brixey was himself captured by Joe Wheeler in the summer of 1864 and executed.[56]

By the beginning of 1865, the entire Cumberland Plateau suffered through seemingly endless raids and counter raids by guerrillas and cavalry forces tasked with defeating them. Some of the violence had a cathartic quality to it; two Campbell County Union soldiers, chafing at their pro-Confederate and major slaveholding neighbor John Kincaid, shot and killed him after he tried to collect on a debt.[57] Some of the violence continued even after the surrender of Lee and Johnston in April 1865. Champ Ferguson nearly

France Cemetery, the final resting place of Champ Ferguson.

killed his old nemesis Tinker Dave Beaty in late April. In May 1865, General Lovell Rousseau offered amnesty to all guerrillas in the Cumberlands, with the exception of Champ Ferguson. Not realizing that he was exempt from the amnesty policy, Ferguson surrendered anyway. He was confined at Nashville, tried by a military tribunal and executed in October.

The end of the guerrilla war did not mean the end of bitterness on the Cumberland Plateau. Farms and homes lay in ruins, families and church communities remained divided, civil society had not been restored and the economy ceased to function. Slaveholders lost their slaves and all the monetary value and social status that slave ownership conferred. Freed people faced violent retribution from angry former slaveholders for asserting their rights as free human beings. A whole generation of young men carried with them the physical and mental scars of a long and bloody civil war. To reconstruct life on the Cumberland Plateau would involve a dramatic change in nearly all facets of life. The final chapter details the struggle of the people along Tennessee's Cumberland Plateau to remake their lives and communities.

RECONSTRUCTING THE CUMBERLAND PLATEAU

As John Muir passed through Jamestown and into Morgan County in 1867, he encountered a "good-looking woman" and her husband, with his "shaggy black hair" further "begrimed" from his iron forge.[1] After sharing lodging and a meal with the curious traveler, the man warned Muir that "although the war was over, walking across the Cumberland Mountains still was far from safe on account of small bands of guerrillas who were in hiding along the roads." Muir did encounter some men who "belonged to the most irreclaimable of the guerrilla bands who, long accustomed to plunder, deplored the coming of peace."[2] But they did not bother Muir, for it was obvious that the man with plants hanging out of his clothes was not worth much.

A few years later, another traveler crossed over the plateau and recorded his observations. After riding horseback for 2,051 miles on the Crossville Circuit, up and down the Cumberland Plateau multiple times, Reverend A.B. Wright jotted down a few notes in his journal about the land and the people he visited: "Fully two thirds of the mountain part of Cumberland County is yet in an uncultivated state...Valuable timber is abundant, coal is plentiful, and I think iron is found in some places... This country lies remote from any railroad."[3] Anticipating criticism of the people in such an "uncultivated" land, Wright insisted that "the native people have been greatly misunderstood by the outside world...[t]hey have done wonderfully well for their advantages."[4] Wright recorded his reflections in 1876 after years of preaching in the Methodist Church throughout the Cumberland Plateau. The Fentress County native saw the devastation and heartbreak of civil war firsthand. And yet he remained hopeful in the period following the war for both a spiritual revival and a worldly reconstruction.

Wright and Muir revealed a place troubled with much conflict and loss. But their reflections also invoked a natural beauty and basic human goodness found along the Cumberland Plateau, from which a new and more prosperous world could emerge. These journeys—roads to someplace else, roads to salvation, roads to progress—symbolized the possibilities for the people on the plateau after the Civil War. Developing those possibilities would prove difficult. Old war wounds would take time to heal. Old social relations torn asunder by war and emancipation would need to be refashioned. People near and far would need to be convinced that new industries and settlement patterns could replace the old.

As was true for the rest of the South, Reconstruction for the people of the Cumberland Plateau meant the development of a new social and labor system in the wake of emancipation. But it also meant the physical reconstruction of the region, with networks of railroads, mines, quarries, factories and factory towns appearing where none existed before. As elsewhere in Reconstruction Appalachia, the people of the Cumberland Plateau would forge new and different kinds of relationships with one another and with the outside world. Some of these relationships would be mutually beneficial, and others would be ruthlessly exploitative. Some would be borne of economics and others religious, educational, philanthropic or experimental.

The expansion of the railroad made possible very different kinds of communities, including utopias like Rugby, Harriman or Monteagle that would provide refuge from the industrial society enabled by those same railroads. With this came a great resettlement, as rural residents moved to growing cities like Knoxville and Chattanooga, to new industrial towns like Oneida and Rockwood or to coal-mining communities like Coalfield or Coalmont. And for those left behind by these changes, there were sites of social justice activism for a new century, as at Highlander Folk School. Meanwhile, others looked to the Cumberland Plateau as a sanctuary to preserve the traditions lost in the Civil War, fulfilling the dream of General Leonidas Polk in creating the University of the South at Sewanee.

The first and most pressing question facing many communities on or near the Cumberland Plateau was the meaning of freedom in the wake

All Saints Chapel at the University of the South at Sewanee.

of emancipation. After all, the social system that produced Southern elites' economic wealth, political power and social status before the war was slavery. Nearly all of the elites along the Cumberland Plateau participated in the slave system, either directly as slaveholders or indirectly as merchants, skilled craftsmen or commercial farmers serving a slave economy. But by the end of 1865, slavery was gone. As the late historian Armstead Robinson remarked, the destruction of slavery was the only permanent result of the creation of the Confederate States of America.[5] Obviously that was not what the secessionists of 1861 intended. But after four long years of civil war, that was the final result: the destruction of the Confederacy meant the restoration of the United States and the elimination of slavery.

Emancipation, which in Tennessee was made official by ratification of a state constitutional amendment on February 22, 1865, simply raised new questions. What would freedom mean for different groups of people? What would freedom mean for the fifty-four people formerly owned by the murdered John Kincaid of Campbell County? What might it mean for George Dibrell's ex-slave who led Federal troops into Sparta? Or for female domestic slaves in Pikeville or Livingston with husbands and children separated by vast distances?

Slavery died hard in Tennessee, as it did everywhere else. More perhaps than in any other state, Tennessee's slave system collapsed as a result of wartime military chaos.[6] A combination of Federal troops, military governor Andrew Johnson, congressional policy, radical Tennessee Unionist soldiers, Tennessee Unionist politicians and the slaves themselves brought the system down. The revolutionary circumstances of military occupation, Confederate resistance and guerrilla war gave room for slaves to make their case for freedom. It also helped push conservative proslavery Unionists into the abolitionist camp, which ultimately destroyed the institution by February 1865. While the Cumberland Plateau contained some of the least slave-populated counties in Tennessee, the institution was still important in the workings of the Confederate army and in sustaining the economy. The Twenty-fifth Tennessee Infantry Regiment muster rolls actually list several free blacks, though with the terms "joined" crossed out by the adjutant general. They were almost certainly joined by slaves of White, Overton, Putnam, Jackson and Fentress Counties and served as laborers, performing vital service in camp and on the battlefield.[7] As such, the slaves were subject to the First Confiscation Act in 1861, which authorized the Union army to seize slaves in the Confederate military service as "contrabands" of war. Later, these "contrabands" would be granted freedom under the Second Confiscation Act of July 1862, and many of them would later enlist in the Union army. Undoubtedly, some of the first slaves to be liberated in Tennessee were those in the Twenty-fifth, especially those running away after the retreat from Mill Springs.

Andrew Johnson and General Don Carlos Buell refused to interfere with the slave system in 1862 for fear of alienating conservative Unionists and because they believed that emancipation was neither militarily necessary nor morally appropriate. Johnson convinced President Lincoln to exempt Tennessee from the Emancipation Proclamation issued on January 1, 1863, because the state was already restored to Federal control. East Tennessee Unionists were of mixed opinions on emancipation. Some came to view it as militarily necessary. Others, like T.A.R. Nelson, vehemently opposed the proclamation and briefly abandoned the Union cause.

Johnson continued to support slavery until sometime in August 1863, when he freed his family slaves in Greeneville and began making speeches calling for not only emancipation but also the enlistment of African Americans in the Union army.[8] It remains a mystery exactly why Johnson changed his mind—perhaps national ambitions tethered him to Lincoln's policy, or perhaps he began to see how desperately the Confederate Army of Tennessee was trying to hold on to the institution. In March 1863, General Braxton Bragg established a depot at McMinnville to house the legions of runaway slaves captured during the months following the Battle of Murfreesboro. Many of these slaves came from the counties west of the plateau. In late May, Bragg feared Federal capture of the depot and moved it to Chattanooga.[9] Bragg suggested, "They could be most usefully employed as laborers, relieving the same number of soldiers."[10] Guerrillas began to take on the role of slave-catchers, forming vigilance committees with the dual task of rounding up Confederate deserters and runaway slaves.[11] Johnson now had all the evidence he needed to make the case for military emancipation in Tennessee. Whatever Johnson's motivations, his change in policy had a profound effect on the institution in Tennessee, especially as it coincided with the Army of the Cumberland's movement toward Chickamauga and Chattanooga in the late summer of 1863.

The acceleration of emancipation policy by both Johnson and the Federal army necessitated the creation of contraband camps to house the men, women and children fleeing from their masters. These camps would appear in the most militarily fortified locations. For the plateau after November 1863, that would mean Chattanooga, just east of the central city above Orchard Knob. Contraband

The grave of Quartermaster Sergeant Thomas Lillard of the First U.S. Colored Heavy Artillery in Alcoa, Tennessee. This unit recruited African Americans from the Cumberland Plateau.

camps quickly developed into shantytowns with heavy concentrations of freed people; after the war, these would become black neighborhoods. By 1870, Chattanooga's black population had more than doubled from the 1860 count of free and enslaved African Americans.[12] Considering the drop in black populations in nearby plateau counties, it is clear that many freed people from the Cumberland Plateau went to Chattanooga during and after the war.

The other major component of emancipation was black enlistment in the Federal army. By the end of the war, 39 percent of military-age black men from Tennessee would serve in the Union army, equaling Missouri and trailing only Kentucky.[13] Most of these enlistees came from Middle and West Tennessee, where slavery was strongest. But in Knoxville, the First U.S. Colored Heavy Artillery recruited primarily from East Tennessee and the Cumberland Plateau. Black troops would appear at key military engagements, including Fort Pillow along the Mississippi River and the pivotal Battle of Nashville in December 1864. They also began to appear for garrison duty in Sparta in 1864, much to the consternation of both Confederates and Unionists alike. Amanda McDowell, a Unionist woman, wrote in her diary in March 1864, "The Yankees are still in Sparta, not only there but have some negro soldiers there too. They were bad enough but when it comes to negroes, Heaven defend us! It is indeed humiliating, but the country deserves to be humiliated. Even to the very dust."[14] McDowell, like many other Tennessee Unionists in the war's later stages, viewed emancipation as the perfect comeuppance for the Confederate master class. "I do not want them to be humiliated through any feeling of revenge, but because I think it will do the people good to learn that they cannot master the world."[15]

Coming to grips with emancipation was difficult for slaveholders and non-slaveholding whites alike. Violence directed at runaway slaves in the last months of the war, echoing similar violence in Kentucky, was intended to either subordinate or expel the black population. African Americans were no longer chattel property, so they no longer conferred the status on slaveholders that they once had. Violence continued after the war, especially as paramilitary organizations like the Ku Klux Klan targeted both blacks and their white Republican political supporters.

Table 4

BLACK POPULATION PERCENTAGE BY COUNTY
BETWEEN 1860 AND 1870

COUNTY	1860 BLACK PERCENTAGE	1870 BLACK PERCENTAGE
Anderson	8%	11%
Bledsoe	18%	15%
Campbell	6%	6%
Claiborne	10%	8%
Fentress	4%	4%
Franklin	26%	20%
Grundy	9%	4%
Hamilton	12%	24%
Jackson	11%	6%
Knox	12%	17%
Marion	11%	13%
Morgan	5%	3%
Overton	9%	5%
Putnam	8%	6%
Rhea	13%	10%
Roane	14%	14%
Scott	2%	1%
Sequatchie	10%	7%
Van Buren	10%	6%
Warren	21%	15%
White	14%	12%

Census returns tell much of the story. In nearly every county along the Cumberland Plateau, the African American percentage of the total population dropped between 1860 and 1870. As the table above demonstrates, some counties experienced dramatic drops in their black populations, including Grundy and Overton Counties, where black percentages were half what they were in 1860. In terms of sheer numbers, the larger slaveholding counties along the western edge of the plateau, such as Warren and Franklin, dropped by the largest amount. Violence committed by "Ku Kluxers," along the southern tier of the counties from Giles east to Franklin, forced many

African Americans to seek safety in Chattanooga or Nashville. Jackson, White, Fentress and Overton Counties, where Confederate guerrillas were so strong during the war, also experienced significant Ku Klux Klan activity.[16] Hamilton County, which includes Chattanooga, experienced a significant increase in its black population percentage, from 12 percent to 24 percent. In some rural areas, African Americans formed their own towns, such as Free Hill near Celina in what was formerly Overton County (now Clay County). Free Hill had its origins in the antebellum era, when a slaveholder named Virginia Hill freed her slaves and gave them land to cultivate.[17] During and after the Civil War, other African Americans moved to the community and engaged in logging and farming. Cumberland County's Tate Town, named for a black Methodist minister, was founded under similar auspices.[18] In other towns, like Sparta, Pikeville and Jasper, freed slaves congregated in certain sections of town for mutual protection against nightriders and to preserve cultural autonomy as a small minority. Violent intimidation of African Americans intensified at the end of the century, with many becoming all-white towns.[19]

Freed people left these counties to search for family, to seek safety in larger towns or simply to seek out better economic opportunities. Interestingly, counties with small concentrations of large slaveholdings—like Campbell or Bledsoe—experienced relatively little drop in black population or percentage. Perhaps the black community was sizable enough to sustain family life in freedom. Many African Americans in Campbell County reported the surname of Kincaid on the 1870 census, which suggests that the large slave community on the Kincaid farm would persist as a viable free black community.[20]

The politics of Reconstruction had a profound effect on the people of the Cumberland Plateau, as it did elsewhere in Tennessee. And just as the Civil War divided the sentiments along the plateau, so, too, did the workings of the Reconstruction government. In 1865, Andrew Johnson became vice president and then president of the United States. Meanwhile, a new state convention passed an emancipation amendment to the state constitution ratified in February, followed shortly afterward by the election of a Republican state assembly dominated by William "Parson" Brownlow of Knoxville. The Brownlow government was a product of wartime disfranchisement provisions that military governor Andrew Johnson applied toward Confederates. Brownlow insisted that ex-Confederates were still disloyal and should continue to be disfranchised. He initiated lawsuits and indictments for treason against Confederates, which convinced many

Confederate supporters on the plateau, like Scott Bledsoe, to leave for Texas.[21] Passage of an ex-Confederate disfranchisement law in 1866 and acceptance of both the Thirteenth and Fourteenth Amendments by July 1866 allowed the state to regain its full representation in Congress again. But Radical Republican rule was imperiled by factionalism among other factors, and Brownlow approved the enfranchisement of African Americans in February 1867, making Tennessee the first Southern state to grant blacks the right to vote.

The appearance of paramilitary violence from the Ku Klux Klan convinced Brownlow to create his own Tennessee State Guard, which policed the polls and helped him secure reelection in 1867.[22] Many officers in the new State Guard had been Union soldiers during the war. Claiborne Beaty, son of Tinker Dave, was appointed captain of the State Guard in 1869 in order to suppress the Ku Klux Klan in Fentress and Overton Counties.[23] Some of the plateau's staunchest Unionists during the war, including Joseph Cooper and William Stokes, would play important roles in the radical government. In 1869, the legislature elected Brownlow to the U.S. Senate, and his successor, Dewitt Clinton Senter, began to change course.[24] Senter, a staunch Unionist, though never as radical as Brownlow, supported calls for a new state constitutional convention to remove the disfranchisement provisions. In 1870, the state ratified a new constitution, effectively ending political Reconstruction and granting political power to Democrats from Middle and West Tennessee. In the East, Republicans continued to dominate, especially as so many Confederate supporters had left—voluntarily or not—in 1865. As in the war, the plateau was on the dividing line between Republican East Tennessee and Democratic Middle Tennessee. By the 1872 presidential election, Campbell, Scott, Fentress, Morgan, Anderson, Roane, Cumberland, Bledsoe, Marion and Hamilton Counties had become Republican strongholds. Overton, Jackson, Putnam, White, Van Buren, Sequatchie, Grundy, Warren and Franklin Counties became some of the most Democratic in the state. Some of the margins along the plateau were almost comically one-sided. Scott County voted for the Republican Ulysses Grant over the Democrat Horace Greeley by a margin of 329 to 7.[25] Jackson and Grundy Counties produced similarly lopsided votes for Greeley.

By the early 1870s, and the establishment of new partisan voting habits on the plateau, enterprising investors began seeking ways to exploit the natural resources of the plateau. As the Reverend A.B. Wright pointed out, resources were plentiful, but railroads to access them were not. Some railroads had penetrated the southern plateau before the war, with the Nashville and Chattanooga passing through the Cowan Tunnel on the way to Stevenson, Alabama. It then crossed the Tennessee River at Bridgeport before rolling into Chattanooga under the bluff of Lookout Mountain. Two short lines from the Nashville and Chattanooga predated the war as well, with a coal railroad going from Cowan to Tracy City and another branch from Tullahoma to McMinnville. Plans were underway to extend the latter line across the Caney Fork to Sparta and to build a line from Bridgeport through Battle Creek and Jasper into the Sequatchie Valley. Neither of these lines was begun before the war. On the other side of the plateau, investors planned to complete a railroad north from Knoxville over Cumberland Mountain at Wheelers Gap and into Kentucky; the line had been built only as far as Clinton in 1861.

Beginning in the 1870s, the line out of Knoxville was extended to Jacksboro and then to Jellico, thereby opening up the coalfields in the Clear Fork Valley of Campbell County for mining. The Sparta line was not completed until 1884, when the Nashville, Chattanooga and St. Louis (NC&STL) Railway purchased it. George Dibrell, after settling his personal financial accounts after the war, invested in the railroad and in the Bon Air coal mines to the east of Sparta. The line was extended from Sparta to Bonair three years after the NC&STL took over the railroad from McMinnville.[26] The Jasper branch of the same railroad was completed in the 1880s and extended all the way through the Sequatchie Valley to Pikeville by 1891.

It would take completion of two major new railroads—the Cincinnati Southern and the Tennessee Central—through the plateau area to make the natural resources available. The Cincinnati Southern Railway completed its route to Chattanooga through Scott, Morgan, Roane and Rhea Counties in 1880. Running parallel to Walden Ridge, the Cincinnati Southern encouraged significant investment in mines, quarries and factories on the eastern Cumberland Plateau. It spawned new towns like Dayton, Oneida, Harriman, Rockwood and the switching yard town of Oakdale and dramatically expanded towns like Sunbright and Huntsville. A promotional brochure written just before completion of the line remarked, "The people of Cincinnati can never have more than a faint conception of the immense and invaluable iron interests of 'East Tennessee,' and it will be amazing, if after sinking sixteen millions of dollars, during these stringent times, in the road, the people refuse to finish the undertaking."[27] The completed road did more to encourage further investment in the region than any other factor.

One other major railroad would cross the Cumberland Plateau by the turn of the twentieth century: the Tennessee Central Railway. Chartered as the Nashville and Knoxville, the road ran east through Lebanon to Cookeville and then ascended the plateau to the resort community of Monterey. It reached Crossville in September 1900 before descending the plateau to Harriman, where it joined the Cincinnati Southern and the East Tennessee, Georgia and Virginia en route to Knoxville.[28] Almost exactly one hundred years after the Walton Road was built over the central Cumberland Plateau as a route from Knoxville to Nashville, a railroad was finally completed along the same journey.

Iron, timber and coal magnates mostly from Pennsylvania, Ohio and Kentucky invested in these railroads through the Cumberland Plateau, though local investors like the former general George Dibrell often owned a partial interest in the roads. Not surprisingly, investors followed up the construction of railroads with a massive investment in the coalfields, iron mines and rock quarries of the region. Timber companies added narrow-gauge roads to reach more difficult stands, especially in the Obed, New and Big South Fork River gorges. Interestingly, many of the Northern investors had traveled through the region during the Civil War and pledged to come back to open up manufacturing or mining operations. Perhaps the most famous was Indianan John Wilder, leader of the Lightning Brigade who established his reputation for bravery at Hoover's Gap and Chickamauga. In the late 1860s, Wilder developed the first blast furnaces in the South—Roane Iron Works—at Rockwood. Wilder's town of Rockwood would grow slowly and steadily as he built his own industrial empire and political career in Chattanooga. When the Cincinnati Southern Railway came through Rockwood in 1880, business accelerated and remained strong well into the twentieth century.

The most important industry to establish itself along the Cumberland Plateau after the 1870s was coal mining. Veins of coal under the Pennsylvanian Age sandstone had beckoned miners for many years. Prior to the Civil War, however, only a handful of coalfields were opened up to mining, with the most profitable run by the Sewanee Mining Company near Tracy City. The small branch line from Cowan to Tracy City set the pattern for railroad-based coal extraction later in the century. Beginning in the 1880s, narrow-gauge short-line railroads were built in all directions from the main trunk lines of the Cincinnati Southern; Nashville, Chattanooga and St. Louis; and the Tennessee Central. It created a genuine coal boom from Campbell to Grundy County and lasted from the 1880s to the 1920s. Some of the new developers were Northern businessmen who used land purchased on the plateau as ways to expand their existing businesses. Justus Stearns, for example, was a timber magnate from Michigan and acquired over fifty thousand acres of land in what was called the "Big Survey." He then developed the Stearns Coal and Timber Company in the Big South Fork of the Cumberland River along the Kentucky-Tennessee border.[29]

The construction of major steel production facilities at Chattanooga and Birmingham accelerated demand for coal, pig iron and coke. In the Sequatchie Valley, the Delaware-based Douglas Coal and Coke Company built hundreds of beehive coke ovens at Dunlap to convert coal into coke for use in the steel mills of Chattanooga. Dayton Coal and Iron Company at Smith's Crossroads in Rhea County opened a similar operation along Richland Creek. At Tracy City, where the first coal mine was built before the war, Arthur St. Clair Colyar of Winchester acquired the old property, formed the Tennessee Coal, Iron and Railroad Company (TCI) and developed the Fiery Gizzard Coke Iron Furnace. Coal-mining communities appeared almost overnight, especially in Campbell, Morgan, Anderson and Grundy Counties. TCI would become the dominant industrial player from Knoxville to Birmingham.

Not everybody benefited from this dramatic Reconstruction on the Cumberland Plateau. Burgeoning industry in the post–Civil War Cumberland Plateau exacerbated class divisions, as mine owners manipulated the weighing process and paid laborers in scrip redeemable only at company stores or for cash on a heavily discounted basis. When miners at Briceville in Anderson County's Coal Creek Valley protested the use of company check-weighmen in 1890, in violation of state law, the Tennessee Coal Mining Company (TCMC) turned to convict leasing to replace the free miners.[30] The Brownlow legislature had established the convict leasing system in 1866, and it expanded across the state over the next several years. Private companies could hire these gangs to perform all kinds of dangerous work and at a very cheap cost. As one historian termed it, convict leasing was "slavery by another name," though its forced laborers were both black and white.[31] TCI was one of the largest exploiters of convict leasing in the state, with hundreds of convicts working along railroads and in mines in Marion and Grundy Counties. It often subleased the convicts to local mining firms, as it did with TCMC at Briceville.

When free Briceville miners protested, the company added insult to injury by dismantling the miners' company-built homes in Briceville and replacing them with a stockade to house the convicts. The use of convicts infuriated both miners and local merchants, who depended on cash wages spent by area miners. Miners petitioned the governor, who, though sympathetic to the miners' cause, noted that the leasing contract lasted until 1895. Frustrated with inaction on the state government's part, the miners surrounded the stockade, captured the convicts and sent them on a train to Knoxville. State militiamen sent to quell the miners' actions served only to amplify the tensions, which exploded into violence.

The Coal Creek War, as it was termed, raged on and off for the next three years. The events drew national attention as the guerrilla-style labor war continued. Miners raided the convict depots at Oliver Springs in October 1891 and freed the prisoners at one point. Similar tensions spread to the Tracy City mines, where TCI actually expanded convict leasing in 1892. Peter Turney, the old arch-secessionist of Franklin County, was elected governor that year. And while Turney, as chief justice of the state Supreme Court, had sided with the coal companies in defense of the sanctity of contract, he understood how costly the system was going forward. Turney let the convict lease with TCI expire in 1895 without renewing it and established a permanent state prison where convicts could mine coal for the state. That prison was located in the town of Petros in Morgan County and was called Brushy Mountain State Prison.

Labor strife continued, especially as working conditions grew increasingly dangerous. In Fratersville, one of the largest mining disasters in American history occurred in 1902 when 216 miners were killed in a mine explosion. Another horrific explosion at nearby Cross Mountain killed 84 miners. The federal government established the Bureau of Mines in 1910 and used the Cross Mountain disaster as one of its first investigative cases. Labor conflict continued up and down the plateau, as miners and mine owners continued to battle over matters of safety, weighing procedures, scrip payments and the right to organize.

After World War I, the mines along Tennessee's Cumberland Plateau began to slow production. Partly, this was a result of much more expansive coalfields now accessible in West Virginia and eastern Kentucky. But it was also a result of the thin Tennessee coal veins being used up. One effect of the drop in coal mine business was the attempt to diversify into other industries or even into convenient "distractions" to drive up retail business. The best-known example of the latter was the famous Scopes Trial at Dayton. As the nearby Richland Creek coking operations slowed in the early 1920s, local businessmen meeting at the Robinson Drugstore proposed that a local teacher named Thomas Scopes deliberately violate the state's new anti-evolution law.[32] The purpose was to attract attention to the town, though

A statue of William Jennings Bryan in front of the Rhea County Courthouse in Dayton, Tennessee.

many devoutly religious residents in the area saw the case as a much more sincere battle between traditional faith and secular modern science. Needless to say, the businessmen got more than they bargained for as the Scopes Trial intensified the culture wars of the 1920s. With nationally known celebrity attorneys William Jennings Bryan and Clarence Darrow converging on the town and Baltimore journalist H.L. Mencken sending his mocking dispatches around the world, Dayton quickly became a global symbol of buffoonish backwardness.[33]

When the Great Depression arrived, coal mining, along with timber operations, came to a halt. Never would either of these industries return to the level of the 1910s. Sensing the economic distress of Tennessee generally, the Roosevelt administration established the Tennessee Valley Authority in 1933 to provide hydroelectric power through a series of dams. The first,

A Civilian Conservation Corps dynamite shack at Frozen Head State Park in Morgan County.

called Norris Dam, was constructed at the edge of Anderson and Campbell Counties and once again altered the landscape. While many residents benefited from the access to cheap electricity and navigation along the river, many others were displaced and forced to find new housing in the middle of the Great Depression. Another jobs program that touched the lives of many people on the plateau was the Civilian Conservation Corps, which helped stop soil erosion and build state and national parks.

Roosevelt also established a cooperative housing community in Cumberland County called the Cumberland Homesteads. Designed to provide modern housing for people struggling in especially hard times, the Homesteads attracted residents from across the plateau to the new community near Crossville. In the meantime, a labor activist named Myles Horton developed an organizing school for distressed miners in Monteagle in Grundy County. Called the Highlander Folk School, Horton modeled his site after the Danish folk school movement and encouraged grass-roots organizing.[34] He also insisted on workers cooperating across the color line. By the 1950s, Highlander had turned more toward training activists in the civil rights movement, with famous activists like Martin Luther King, Rosa Parks and Septima Clark joining legions of lesser-known local activists from across the South.

While the Cumberland Plateau attracted significant investment in mining and manufacturing interests, it also provided a space for those trying to escape this new industrial world. Dreamers and utopians of all kinds sought refuge on the plateau, some with lasting significance and others fleeting. Just as with industry and mining, the plateau sanctuary ideal predated the Civil War. Many of the early sanctuaries were the healing springs and summer resorts at places like Bon Air Springs and Beersheba Springs. Originally built by Christopher Haufmann in 1840, Bon Air Hotel was purchased by John B. Rogers, who owned the property into the Civil War. A sincere Unionist, Rogers was a continual target for Bledsoe's guerrillas, who eventually destroyed the resort buildings during the war. Bon Air would be developed as a coal mine community later on. Beersheba, long owned by Armfield, also suffered destruction and looting during the Civil War, including from many deserters and Unionists.[35] Newer resorts like those at Monterey beckoned summer travelers from Nashville, Knoxville and Chattanooga.

Other sanctuaries served deeper purposes than mere leisure. The most lasting sanctuary on the Cumberland Plateau was a university, dubbed the University of the South at Sewanee. Bishop Leonidas Polk and members from Episcopal dioceses across the South first established the seminary on land

2E   75

HIGHLANDER FOLK SCHOOL
1932-1962

In 1932, Myles Horton and Don West founded
Highlander Folk School, located 1/2 mile north of
this site. It quickly became one of the few schools
in the South committed to the cause of organized
labor, economic justice, and an end to racial
segregation. Courses included labor issues,
literacy, leadership, and non-violent desegre-
gation strategies, with workshops led by Septima
Clark. The Rev. Dr. Martin Luther King, Jr., Rosa
Parks, John Lewis, and Eleanor Roosevelt found
inspiration for the modern civil rights movement
there. Opponents of its causes tried to close
the school.
Continued

TENNESSEE HISTORICAL COMMISSION

The original site of the Highlander Folk School, founded by Myles
Horton and attended by Martin Luther King and Rosa Parks at one
point during the civil rights movement.

owned by the Sewanee Mining Company. It served distinctly Southern
sectarian purposes, with founding bishop James H. Otey hoping that it
would "materially aid the South to resist and repel a fanatical domination
which seeks to rule over us."[36] The war interrupted the school's construction,
with Illinois troops destroying the cornerstone at one point in 1863. In 1867,
John Armfield purchased the current site of the university and endowed
a significant annual donation to the school for its operation. Confederate

general E. Kirby Smith, chief of ordnance Josias Gorgas and chaplain in the Army of Tennessee Charles Todd Quintard helped re-found the University of the South in 1867. Steeped in the tradition of the Confederacy and a bastion of the Lost Cause into the middle of the twentieth century, Sewanee prospered as a liberal arts college, a seminary and a boarding school.

Another remarkable sanctuary to appear on the Cumberland Plateau was the English utopian community of Rugby. Thomas Hughes, an English social reformer, purchased land in northern Morgan County, where he established a colony based on cooperative enterprise and farming. Completion of the Cincinnati Southern Railway made Rugby an attractive destination for the new settlement. Most of the inhabitants of Rugby were the children of British aristocracy, and they quickly developed dozens of Victorian-style buildings to serve as libraries, schools, churches and homes. Over three hundred people lived in Rugby at its peak. A "Gentleman's Swimming Hole" was a favorite attraction, as was a somewhat more remote "Ladies' Bathing Place." The cooperative agricultural system struggled on the harsh plateau soil, however, and the colony had begun to decline by the end of the 1880s.[37]

Rugby was far from the only planned utopia, though it was arguably the most elegant. Religious reformers associated with the temperance movement founded colonies on the plateau as well, including Monteagle and Harriman.[38] A Scotsman named John Moffat established a normal school on the Monteagle site in Grundy County. His community followed the Chautauqua tradition, with schools, church revivals, music and festivals attracting widespread attention. Harriman served a more conservative purpose as a planned temperance town and industrial settlement. Founded by Frederick Gates of New York, the East Tennessee Land Company purchased the Harriman tract near the junction of the Cincinnati Southern and the East Tennessee, Virginia and Georgia Railway. Named for a Civil War colonel from New Hampshire named William Harriman, who traveled through the Emory Gap area during the war, Harriman grew into a sizable industrial town in the 1890s. The East Tennessee Land Company failed in just a few years, but the town continued to prosper thanks to its proximity to the railroads.[39] The town was held up as an example of industrialism without the associated vice of other nearby communities.

Some of the new communities established on the plateau after the Civil War were geared entirely toward enticing European immigrants to settle. Wartburg had been a modest success in the 1840s, but new investors saw opportunities for immigrants fleeing the rapid economic changes in 1860s Europe. Bruno Gerndt and M.H. Allardt had established a community in

The land office for German immigrants in Allardt, Tennessee.

Michigan for German immigrants. They sought a new location in Tennessee and established the Allardt community in 1881, shortly after the Cincinnati Southern was completed. Several of the German immigrants came from Michigan and others directly from Germany. Though smaller than Rugby,

Allardt was more successful; the main street named Michigan Avenue testifies to the original colony site.[40] In Grundy County, E.H. Plumacher and John Hitz of the Swiss Emigration Society founded a settlement for Swiss families fleeing economic difficulties. Named Gruetli in honor of a place of importance in Swiss national history, the community reached about one hundred families before leveling off. A neighboring Swiss community called Laager also encouraged migrants to settle in the area near Savage Gulf.[41]

Though we often think of Reconstruction as an era, corresponding to the ten years or so after the Civil War, it is more accurate to describe Reconstruction as a process. An entire social, economic, racial and political system was destroyed amidst a bloody civil war. For much of the South, the central task at the heart of Reconstruction was to mark out new meanings of freedom and citizenship in the wake of emancipation. For people along the Cumberland Plateau, emancipation raised similar sorts of questions, albeit to a small degree. On the plateau, Reconstruction also meant the physical process of rebuilding communities, infrastructure and farms, much of which lay in ruins after the destruction caused by conventional and guerrilla war. The land, too, needed to revitalize, as places like Cumberland Gap had been denuded of trees during the war. Most important would be the large-scale industrialization of the region, made possible by railroads and the presence of valuable coal, iron and timber resources. This would take a second toll on the landscape that would require another kind of environmental reconstruction in the mid-twentieth century. With such permanent change wrought by the Civil War and its aftermath, the Cumberland Plateau is still in the process of reconstructing itself today.

CONCLUSION

B illy Hull barely survived the Civil War. Shortly before the war ended, Hull traded a cow for a rifle from a neighbor named Jim Stepp. But Stepp changed his mind, decided he wanted his gun back and went over to the Hull place to "recover" his silver rifle. An angry Billy Hull confronted Stepp and forced him to return the gun that had been delivered as part of the original deal. Stepp then turned to a Unionist guerrilla named Riley Piles and told him that Hull was helping to arm the Confederate bushwhackers. Piles rounded up his fellow Union guerrillas, found Hull with a friend and shot them both. The friend died, and Hull barely survived a gunshot wound to his eye.[1]

After the war officially ended, Hull sought revenge. He found Jim Stepp in Kentucky, cussed him out and shot him dead. Hull was satisfied and returned to his quiet farm in Overton County, where he and his wife had five sons. The third son was named Cordell in honor of a family friend in Scott County. As Billy entered the timber business and moved closer to Celina, Cordell Hull went to school, studied hard and then went to law school at Cumberland University. Ascending the ranks of the Tennessee Democratic Party, Cordell Hull eventually became President Franklin D. Roosevelt's secretary of state. His lasting legacy was cemented in 1943, when he drafted the charter of the United Nations. Two years later, the United Nations came into being, and Hull was awarded the Nobel Peace Prize. Quite an ironic twist for a man born to a father swallowed up in the guerrilla violence of the Civil War on the Cumberland Plateau.

The birthplace of Cordell Hull.

A few miles east of Hull's birthplace, near the old McGinnis camp, another notable figure grew up. Grandson of Union soldier Uriah York, Alvin C. York joined the U.S. Army in 1917 and became the most decorated U.S. soldier in the entire war. He used his newfound fame to advance education on the plateau, including establishing the Alvin York Institute in Jamestown.

156

Cordell Hull is known as the father of the United Nations. *Courtesy of United States Library of Congress.*

Heading a bit farther in each direction, one finds the roots of political titans in the late twentieth century. To the west, near where the Caney Fork flows into the Cumberland, were the stomping grounds of two Gore brothers who fought on different sides—Isaac Gore joined Company B of the Twenty-fifth Tennessee Infantry (CSA) in 1861, and his younger brother Overton Gore joined the Eighth Tennessee Mounted Infantry (USA) in January 1865. Their brother Claiborn Charles Gore had a grandson named Albert Gore Sr., the Tennessee senator and father of Albert Gore Jr., future vice president of the United States. To the east, in Scott County, was a dynasty of a different party. Though born in Somerset, Kentucky, Howard Baker Sr. settled in Huntsville, ran a newspaper and became a Republican representative in Congress. His son, Howard Baker Jr., became a prominent senator and Senate majority leader after 1980. Known as one of the great gentlemen of the Senate and a great compromiser, Howard Baker was one of the most popular and respected politicians of his time. His successor in Congress was John Duncan Sr., who had even deeper Scott County roots. A direct ancestor, Henry Duncan, served in a Unionist Home Guard unit called the

The grave of Sergeant Alvin C. York, the most decorated U.S. soldier in World War I. Camp McGinnis was near this site.

East Tennessee National Guard.[2] John "Jimmy" Duncan Jr. continues to represent Tennessee's Second District in Congress today.

The Civil War established important legacies everywhere. Some of those legacies came in the form of vast battlefields. In other cases, it was a partisan tradition that continued unabated into and through the twentieth century. The Cumberland Plateau has seen both—spectacular park views at Lookout Mountain and deeply partisan political traditions that produced leading national figures in the Democratic and Republican Parties over the next century. But in many ways, the Civil War remains hidden in the life of the Cumberland Plateau. As new retirement communities develop on the plateau, drawing residents from across the country, fewer residents of the plateau can claim direct ties to the region's Civil War past.

And yet, the stories of war, division, privation and survival that defined the Civil War along the Cumberland Plateau still beckon listeners today. National Park sites at Cumberland Gap, Big South Fork, Obed Wild and Scenic River—and, of course, Chickamauga and Chattanooga National Military Park—incorporate the Civil War story into their cultural programming, though to different degrees. Tennessee's wonderful state park system includes many units on the Cumberland Plateau that reveal a Civil War story, including Pickett, Cumberland Mountain, South Cumberland, Frozen Head, Cordell Hull Birthplace, Indian Mountain, Cove Mountain, Alvin C. York Birthplace, Rock Island, Fall Creek Falls and the great Cumberland Trail. A flurry of interest in guerrilla warfare has drawn increasing attention to the region that produced Champ Ferguson. But much of it remains largely invisible.

My hope is that this book helps to piece together the story of the Civil War along Tennessee's Cumberland Plateau and place it within the context of the plateau's larger natural and human history. While this book offers an interpretation of the Civil War on the plateau, one defined by a complex topography and social networks within rural neighborhoods, there is clearly much more room for exploration.

NOTES

INTRODUCTION

1. Tarrant, *Wild Riders*, 39–40.
2. Report of Col. William A. Hoskins, Twelfth Kentucky Infantry, *Original Records of the War of the Rebellion* (hereafter cited as *OR*) 1(4), 203–05.
3. Brents, *Patriots and Guerillas*, 102–03.
4. Blankenship, *Fiddles in the Cumberlands*.
5. Ibid., preface.
6. Christian and McNeill, *Maps of Time*.

CHAPTER 1

1. Killebrew, *Tennessee*, 6.
2. Dr. E.M. Wight, "A People Without Consumption: The Cumberland Tableland. Part 2," *Scientific American: Supplement Volumes for Scientific American* (1885).
3. There are several explanations for the origin of the Fiery Gizzard's name, including a description of an early blast furnace and various Native American stories. For an excellent description of the Fiery Gizzard Cove, see Manning, *Historic Cumberland Plateau*, 257–78.
4. For a detailed explanation of the challenge of road construction along the plateau and a great overview of the geology of the state, see Moore, *Geologic Trip*.

5. For a classic natural history and geography of Appalachia, see Brooks, *The Appalachians.*

6. Houk, *Great Smoky Mountains.*

7. Byerly, *Last Billion Years,* 142–46.

8. Though he focuses mostly on Kentucky, Harry Caudill offered one of the first sustained analyses of the Cumberland Plateau in Caudill and Udall, *Night Comes to the Cumberlands.*

9. Manning, *Historic Cumberland Plateau,* 5–13.

10. Luther, *Our Restless Earth,* 43–53.

11. Ibid., 36–41.

12. Ray, *Middle Tennessee*; Ash, *Middle Tennessee Society.*

13. Moore, *Geologic Trip,* 183–200.

14. Williams, *Appalachia,* 62.

15. Luther, *Our Restless Earth,* 54–62.

16. Miller, "Where and Why of Pine Mountain," 353–71.

17. Byerly, *Last Billion Years,* 120–126.

18. Luther, *Our Restless Earth,* 58.

19. The best modern atlas to identify the creeks and landforms of the Cumberland Plateau is Delorme, *Tennessee Atlas & Gazetteer.*

20. For county data, see Chuck Sutherland's flickr photo of "Tennessee Cave Survey," *Tennessee Cave Survey,* http://www.subworks.com/tcs (accessed December 24, 2014).

21. Manning, *Historic Cumberland Plateau,* 187–90.

22. Plemons, "United States Saltpeter Cave Survey," 11–17.

23. Smith, "In Quest of a Supply," 96–111.

24. McDade, *Natural Arches Big South Fork.*

25. An essential collection of landforms, including arches, can be found on the Tennessee Landforms website, created by Tom Dunigan, "Tennessee Landforms," December 12, 2014, http://tnlandforms.us/landforms.

26. The best general history of the Sequatchie Valley is Raulston and Livingood, *Sequatchie.*

27. For a wonderful and recently written novel that explores the lives of ordinary people in the Sequatchie Valley during the Civil War, see Wade, *Broken Valley.*

28. For an entertaining history of geology and science in general see Bryson, *A Short History,* 63–78.

29. Byerly, *Last Billion Years,* 177–78.

30. Ibid., 44–45.

31. Smithsonian Institution Archives, Record Unit 7301, Troost, Gerard, 1776–1850, Gerard Troost Manuscript and Related Notes, Papers and Drawings.
32. Byerly, *Last Billion Years,* 47–50.
33. Safford, *Geology of Tennessee,* 136–37.
34. Wegener, *Origin of Continents and Oceans.*
35. Byerly, *Last Billion Years.*
36. Luther, *Our Restless Earth,* 1–9.
37. Ryder, "Cincinnati Arch Province."
38. Byerly, *Last Billion Years,* 101–14.
39. Ibid., 51–54.
40. Ibid., 101–04.
41. Ibid., 60.
42. Ibid., 142–46.
43. Moore, *Geologic Trip Across Tennessee,* 40.
44. Byerly, *Last Billion Years,* 166.
45. Manning, *Historic Cumberland Plateau,* 15–18.
46. Ibid., 250.
47. Dillard, *Standing Stone.*
48. Crawford, *Ashe County's Civil War.*
49. Williams, *Appalachia.*
50. Kenzer, *Kinship and Neighborhood.*
51. For an excellent study of a deeply divided region of Appalachia, see Sarris, *A Separate Civil War.*

CHAPTER 2

1. Montell, *Don't Go Up Kettle Creek,* 41–42.
2. This point is driven home in great detail in Dunn, *Civil War in Southern Appalachian Methodism.*
3. For a great overview of early settlement in Kentucky and Tennessee, see Aron, *How the West Was Lost,* and Ray, *Middle Tennessee.*
4. Kenny, *Peaceable Kingdom Lost.*
5. Caruso, *Appalachian Frontier.*
6. Aron, *How the West Was Lost*; Ramage and Watkins, *Kentucky Rising.*
7. Caruso, *Appalachian Frontier,* 62–82.
8. Goodspeed, *History of Tennessee Illustrated,* 847.
9. Biggers, *United States of Appalachia,* 45–66.
10. Barksdale, *Lost State of Franklin.*

11. Williams, *Appalachia*, 19–82.

12. Abernethy, *From Frontier to Plantation in Tennessee.*

13. Bergeron, Keith and Ash, *Tennesseans & Their History*, 47–57.

14. Ibid., 113–17.

15. Authors of a recent atlas on the Cumberland settlements argue, persuasively, that the term "Avery Trace" was not used during the late eighteenth or early nineteenth centuries to refer to the turnpike west of Clinch Mountain. However, it has entered common usage for this turnpike today, even if it was officially known as the North Carolina Military Trace west of Blaine. Drake, *Founding of the Cumberland Settlements.*

16. Dickinson, "The Walton Road," 126–37.

17. Bullard, *Cumberland County's First Hundred Years*, 23.

18. Wirt, *Upper Cumberland of Pioneer Times*, 20–24.

19. Raulston and Livingood, *Sequatchie*, 115–34; Hannah, *Confederate Action in Franklin County*, 1–8.

20. Arbuckle, *Cowan Pusher District.*

21. Jones, *Gateway to the Confederacy*, 13–35.

22. Bullard, *Cumberland County's First Hundred Years*, 68–69.

23. "Eighth Population Census of the United States," 1860.

24. All are in Fentress County, except the three Frost brothers from White County. "Eighth Population Census Manuscripts—1860."

25. "Eighth Population Census of the United States," 1860.

26. White County Minute Books, 1835–1841.

27. Ogle, *Biographies of the Cumberland Region*, 474; censuses of 1810, 1850 and 1860.

28. I am indebted to Merritt Blakeslee, author of a forthcoming work on the Civil War in the Lower Cumberland Plateau, for this observation. Also see Blevins, *Sequatchie Valley Soldiers.*

29. "Eighth Population Census of the United States," 1860.

30. Hogue, *History of Fentress County*, 37–38.

31. Freytag and Ott, *History of Morgan County.*

32. Goodspeed, *History of Tennessee.*

33. Williams, *Legends and Stories of White County*, "Thomas Eastland."

34. Montell, *Don't Go Up Kettle Creek.*

35. Crawford, *Ashe County's Civil War*; Sarris, *A Separate Civil War.*

36. "Eighth Population Census of the United States," 1860, Slave Schedules.

37. Baptist, *Half Has Never Been Told*, 239–40.

38. Whites, "Forty Shirts and a Wagonload of Wheat," 56–78.

39. "Eighth Population Census of the United States," 1860.

40. McCurry, *Masters of Small Worlds*.

41. Groce, *Mountain Rebels*; Inscoe and McKinney, *Heart of Confederate Appalachia*.

42. Atkins, *Parties, Politics, and the Sectional Conflict*.

43. Raulston and Livingood, *Sequatchie*, 72–93.

Chapter 3

1. Resolutions printed in Hannah, *Confederate Action in Franklin County*, 2.

2. Ibid., 3.

3. Roy, *Scott County in the Civil War*, 1.

4. Crawford, *Ashe County's Civil War*.

5. McCurry, *Masters of Small Worlds*.

6. Oakes, *Freedom National*.

7. Bergeron, Keith and Ash, *Tennesseans & Their History*, 132–35.

8. *Athens Post*, February 15, 1861.

9. Ibid.

10. Ibid., February 22, 1861.

11. On Isham Harris, see Elliott, *Isham G. Harris of Tennessee*.

12. Blankenship, *Fiddles in the Cumberlands*, 49–50.

13. Schroeder, "Writings of a Tennessee Unionist," 246.

14. Crofts, *Reluctant Confederates*.

15. For a chart listing all county votes in June 1861, see Appendix C in Fisher, *War at Every Door*.

16. All election data found in Campbell, *Attitude of Tennesseans*, 265–94.

17. For military rosters and official regimental histories, see Tennessee Historical Commission, *Tennesseans in the Civil War*; "Eighth Population Census Manuscripts—1860"; "Eighth Slave Census Manuscripts—1860."

18. TICW regimental histories have been transcribed by "Tennessee and the Civil War," *Tennessee and the Civil War*, http://www.tngenweb.org/civilwar (accessed December 23, 2014).

19. Connelly, *Army of the Heartland*, 25–45.

20. Ibid., 46–77.

21. Regiment, company and census data are cross-referenced with "Compiled Service Records," Fold3, http://www.fold3.com (accessed December 23, 2014); "Civil War Data," *American Civil War Research Database*, http://www.civilwardata.com/active/index.html (accessed December 23, 2014); "Eighth Population Census Manuscripts—1860"; "Eighth Slave Census Manuscripts—1860"; "Tennessee and the Civil War."

22. For the Tullos Rangers, see *Athens Post*, July 12, 1861; for Bledsoe County soldiers generally, see Robnett, *Bledsoe County*.
23. McKnight, *Confederate Outlaw Champ Ferguson*, 24.
24. "Eighth Population Census Manuscripts—1860"; "Civil War Data."
25. Harrison, *Civil War in Kentucky*, 14–33.
26. Fisher, *War at Every Door*, 41–61.
27. Miller, *Civil War and Campbell County*, 9–11.
28. Civil War Service Records, "Joseph A. Cooper" in Company A, First Regiment East Tennessee Infantry (USA), Fold3.com (accessed December 4, 2014). Record shows enlistment on August 2, 1861, to expire on October 31, 1861. "Civil War Data"; "Compiled Service Records."
29. O'Neal, "Civil War on the Upper Cumberland Plateau."
30. Tennessee Historical Commission, *Tennesseans in the Civil War*.
31 Hafendorfer, *Battle of Wild Cat Mountain*, 36.
32. Fisher, *War at Every Door*, 41–61.
33. F.K. Zollicoffer to Samuel Cooper, November 7, 1861, *OR* 1(4), 527.
34. Landon C. Haynes to President Davis, November 8, 1861, *OR* 1(4), 529–30.
35. Special Orders Number 216, November 11, 1861, *OR* 1(4), 538.
36. Ellis, *Thrilling Adventures of Daniel Ellis*.
37. Bullard, *Cumberland County's First Hundred Years*, 55.
38. Harvey, *Tales of the Civil War Era*, 50–51.
39. Thomas Bramelette to General George Thomas, November 11, 1861, at Camp Wolford, *OR* 1(4), 352–53.
40. Ibid.
41. Sanders, *Battle of Mill Springs*.

CHAPTER 4

1. Report of Colonel Henry A. Hambright, Seventy-ninth Pennsylvania Infantry, *OR* 10(1), 920–21.
2. Negley to General Ormsby Mitchell, June 8, 1862, *OR* 10(1), 920.
3. Report of E. Kirby Smith, June 8, 1862, *OR* 10(1), 921.
4. Report of Brigadier General Jas. S. Negley, June 8, 1862, *OR* 10(1), 920.
5. James Negley to Governor Andrew Johnson at Shelbyville, Tennessee, June 12, 1862, *OR* 10(1), 920.
6. Ibid.
7. Report of E. Kirby Smith, June 10, 1862, *OR* 10(1), 922.

8. See essay by Gerald J. Prokopowicz in Jones, *Gateway to the Confederacy*, ch. 2.
9. For an excellent summary of operations in Tennessee and Kentucky after Shiloh and before Chickamauga, see Hess, *Banners to the Breeze*.
10. I am indebted to James Lewis, ranger at Stones River National Battlefield Park, for illustrating Chattanooga's vulnerabilities so clearly.
11. Jones, *Gateway to the Confederacy*.
12. Mcdonough, *Shiloh—In Hell before Night*.
13. Report of James P.T. Carter, March 23, 1862, *OR* 10(1), 19.
14. Ibid.
15. Report of E. Kirby Smith, March 15, 1862, *OR* 10(1), 21.
16. Ibid., March 28, 1862, *OR* 10(1), 50.
17. Ibid.
18. Quoted in Fisher, *War at Every Door*, 105.
19. For a discussion of changing Confederate military policy in East Tennessee in 1862, see Fisher, *War at Every Door*, 102–21.
20. George W. Morgan to Honorable E.M. Stanton, May 19, 1862, *OR* 10(2), 204.
21. Ibid., May 24, 1862, *OR* 10(2), 213.
22. Hess, *Civil War in the West*.
23. For a good summary of Buell's 1862 move toward Chattanooga, see Hess, *Banners to the Breeze*, 6–18.
24. Hurst, *Nathan Bedford Forrest*.
25. Ramage, *Rebel Raider*.
26. Hess, *Banners to the Breeze*, 21.
27. For a great account of the response of civilians to the soldiers, see Noe, *Perryville*, 30.
28. A good description of Morgan's evacuation of Cumberland Gap is in the *New York Times*, October 11, 1862.
29. Moses Joseph Nichols to his parents, August 3, 1862, from Camp Chattanooga in WPA Civil War Records, vol. 3, 121–23, printed in Jones, *Annotations on the Civil*, 14. According to the 1860 census, Moses Nichols's parents owned $2,000 worth of real estate and $2,895 worth of personal property. Typically, that amount of personal property would indicate slave ownership, though D.H. Nichols does not show up on the slave census for the eleventh district of Putnam County. See Eighth Census, Putnam County, Tennessee, Population Manuscripts, 1860.
30. Ibid.
31. McDowell, *Fiddles in the Cumberlands*, 134–35.
32. Ibid., 134.

33. Hess, *Banners to the Breeze*, 56–60.

34. Jones, "Civil War in Van Buren County," 58.

35. *Civil War Diary of Darius Clark*, entry for September 1–2, 1862, Tennessee State Library and Archives.

36. Noe, *Perryville*.

37. Daniel, *Days of Glory*.

38. Cozzens, *No Better Place to Die*.

39. Special Order No. 1, HQQRS, Department No. 2, Sparta, Tenn., September 5, 1862, *OR* 16(2), 797–98.

40. Major General Sam Jones to His Excellency Governor Isham Harris, September 21, 1862, *OR* 16(1), 862.

41. Ibid., October 17, 1862, *OR* 16(2), 862.

42. William G. Swan to President Jefferson Davis, October 21, 1862, *OR* 16(2), 953.

43. *Chattanooga Daily Rebel*, November 6, 1862.

44. Pillow, January 18, 1863, *OR* 4(2), 362.

45. Bradley, *Tullahoma*.

46. Report of William P. Sanders, *OR* 23(1), 386–89.

47. Bragg quoted in Daniel Crofts, "Across the Cumberlands," *New York Times*, August 16, 2013.

48. Diary of Henry Campbell, *Three Years in the Saddle*, August 16, 1863, transcribed and digitized at Wabash College, http://replica. palni.edu/cdm/compoundobject/collection/saddle/id/417/rec/1 (accessed December 10, 2014).

49. Campbell, *Three Years in the Saddle*, August 19, 1863.

50. Powell, *Chickamauga Campaign*.

51. White, *Bushwhacking on a Grand Scale*.

52. Cozzens, *Shipwreck of Their Hopes*.

53. Woodworth, *Six Armies in Tennessee*.

54. Cozzens, *Shipwreck of Their Hopes*, 19.

55. Connelly, *Autumn of Glory*, 137–360.

56. Cozzens, *Shipwreck of Their Hopes*, 48–65.

57. Hess, *Knoxville Campaign*.

58. Cozzens, *Shipwreck of Their Hopes*, 257–377.

59. Hess, *Knoxville Campaign*.

CHAPTER 5

1. Stories of the incident appear in several sources, including Tennessee County Court Minutes, 1866–1869; "Julia A. Marcum," letter written by her on August 7, 1926, Kentucky Historical Society; Smith, *Dusty Bits of the Forgotten Past*, 159–60; Roy, *Scott County in the Civil War*; McKnight, "Julia Marcum's War," *New York Times*, September 11, 2011.
2. Sutherland, *Savage Conflict*, preface.
3. Mackey, *Uncivil War*, 9.
4. Sutherland, *Savage Conflict*, xii.
5. Whites, "Forty Shirts and a Wagonload of Wheat."
6. C.B. Ryan to Andrew Johnson, July 9, 1861, *Papers of Andrew Johnson*, vol. 4, 553–54.
7. Ibid.
8. G.W. Keith to Andrew Johnson, July 12, 1861, *Papers of Andrew Johnson*, vol. 4, 560–61.
9. S.S. Bush to Andrew Johnson, *Papers of Andrew Johnson*, vol. 4, 580.
10 Ibid.
11. A.A. Swope and twenty others to Governor Harris, October 14, 1861, *OR* 52(2), 178–81.
12. Simon Bolivar Buckner to Governor Harris, October 17, 1861, *OR* 52(2), 178–81.
13. J.M. Morgan recollection, *Confederate Veteran*, April 1909.
14. Trial of Champ Ferguson, testimony of David Beaty printed in the *Nashville Union*, July 21–22, 1865.
15. Sanderson, *County Scott and Its Mountain Folk*, 189–90.
16. Roy, *Scott County in the Civil War*, 1.
17. Ibid.
18. Dickinson, *Morgan County*, 35–37.
19. Report of D. Ledbetter, February 5, 1862, *OR* 7(1), 118–19.
20. Baggett, *Homegrown Yankees*, 41.
21. Report of E. Kirby Smith, March 28, 1862, *OR* 10(1), 50.
22. Temple, *Notable Men of Tennessee*, 94.
23. See Clift Family Papers, ca. 1820–1968, Tennessee State Library and Archives, Nashville, especially "Sketches—The Civil War in Eastern Tennessee and How It Affected the Clift Family of Hamilton County."
24. For an excellent description of Clift's activities in Scott County and the guerrilla war in general, see O'Neal, "The Civil War...On the Cumberland Plateau in Tennessee," published in the Winter and Spring

1986 newsletters of the Scott County Historical Society and reprinted as "FNB Chronicles" at http://tngenweb.org/scott/fnb_v7n3_the_civil_war.htm, created September 6, 2008 (accessed December 1, 2014).

25. Ibid.

26. Report of Colonel William Clift, October 28, 1862, *OR* 16(1), 858–59.

27. J.F. Belton, Assistant Adjutant General to Colonel S.J. Smith, August 23, 1862, *OR* 16(2), 774.

28. McKnight, *Confederate Outlaw: Champ Ferguson*, 49.

29. Ibid., 45.

30. *Nashville Union*, October 21, 1865.

31. Mays, *Cumberland Blood*, 59.

32. Eighth U.S. Census, Overton County.

33. Brents, *Patriots and Guerillas*, 66.

34. Ramage, *Rebel Raider*.

35. Siburt, "Colonel John Hughs," 88.

36. Bragg, Order #217, in Fold3, Civil War Service Records, August 14, 1863.

37. Baggett, *Homegrown Yankees*, 87–102.

38. General William Rosecrans to Lieutenant LeRoy Fitch, February 15–16, 1863, *OR* 23(2), 71–72.

39. Rosecrans to Henry Halleck, February 22, 1863, *OR* 23(2), 81.

40. For extended correspondence regarding the Cumberland River campaign, see *OR* 23(2), 130–60.

41. Crook to General James Garfield, March 21, 1863, *OR* 23(2), 157–58.

42. "Tackett Cemetery" in *Cemeteries of the Big South Fork National River and Recreation Area*, National Park Service brochure.

43. McDowell, *Fiddles in the Cumberlands*, July 25, 1863, 203.

44. Ibid.

45. Report of George G. Dibrell, August 18, 1863, *OR* 23(1), 846–68.

46. McDowell, *Fiddles in the Cumberlands*, August 17, 1863, 210; also see Report of G.G. Dibrell, August 17, 1863, *OR* 30(2), 527–28.

47. Baggett, *Homegrown Yankees*, 141.

48. Report of Lieutenant James P. Brownlow, November 29, 1863, *OR* 31(1), 591.

49 McDowell, *Fiddles in the Cumberlands*, December 1, 1863, 223.

50. Report of John M. Hughs, February 22, 1864, *OR* 32(1), 56.

51. Whiteaker, "Battle of Dug Hill," C–8.

52. Dudney, "Civil War in White County," 35–37.

53. Report of William B. Stokes, February 22, 1864, *OR* 32(1), 416–17.

54. Jim Nicholson, "New Light on Skirmish Here (Tracy City, TN)," *Grundy County Herald*, 1977.

55. Richard M. Edwards to Andrew Johnson, *Papers of Andrew Johnson*, vol. 6, September 30, 1863.
56. Correspondence with Merritt Blakeslee, whose forthcoming work on the Civil War in the Lower Cumberland Plateau addresses Brixey's activities in greater detail.
57. *Knoxville Whig and Rebel Ventilator*, February 22, 1865.

CHAPTER 6

1. Muir and Jenkins, *Thousand-Mile Walk*, 22.
2. Ibid., 29.
3. Wright, *Autobiography*, 155.
4. Ibid.
5. Robinson, Reidy and Fields, *Bitter Fruits of Bondage*.
6. The best history of emancipation in Tennessee is Cimprich, *Slavery's End in Tennessee*.
7. See the Compiled Service Record for Micajah Scott of the Twenty-fifth Tennessee Infantry.
8. See especially Johnson's speech at Franklin, *Papers of Andrew Johnson*, vol. 6.
9. Braxton Bragg to Samuel Cooper, May 24, 1863, *OR* 23(2), 850.
10. Ibid. For the original order establishing depots, see General Orders No. 25, *OR* 2(5), 844–45.
11. Cimprich, *Slavery's End in Tennessee*, 30.
12. Eighth and Ninth U.S. Population Censuses, 1860 and 1870.
13. Berlin, Reidy and Rowland, *Freedom*.
14. McDowell, *Fiddles in the Cumberland*, March 26, 1864, 233.
15. Ibid.
16. Birdwell and Dickinson, *Rural Life and Culture*, 109.
17. Walid Kharif, "Free Hill," in *Tennessee Encyclopedia of History and Culture*, available online at http://www.tennesseeencyclopedia.net/entry.php?rec=513.
18. See Walid Kharif in Birdwell and Dickinson, *Rural Life and Culture*, 112–13.
19. Ibid., 111.
20. See Ninth U.S. Census, Population Manuscripts, 1870.
21. Tracy McKenzie discusses this at length for post–Civil War Knoxville. It happened on the Cumberland Plateau as well. McKenzie, *Lincolnites and Rebels*.
22. Severance, *Tennessee's Radical Army*.
23. Hogue, *Mark Twain's Obedstown*, 41.

24. For a detailed discussion of the collapse of Brownlow's government, see the PhD dissertation Hardy, "'Fare Well to All Radicals.'"
25. *Knoxville Daily Chronicle*, November 8, 1872.
26. *New York Times*, April 3, 1884.
27. *Panoramic View of the Cincinnati Southern Railway*, 7.
28. Bullard, *Cumberland County's First Hundred Years*, 111.
29. *Mining in the Big South Fork*, National Park Service brochure.
30. For an excellent study on the Coal Creek War and labor strife on the Cumberland Plateau coalfields generally, see Shapiro, *A New South Rebellion*.
31. Blackmon, *Slavery by Another Name*.
32. Kazin, *A Godly Hero*, 286–88.
33. Larson, *Summer for the Gods*.
34. Glen, *Highlander*.
35. Private correspondence with Merritt Blakeslee, who is working on a forthcoming book on the Civil War in the Lower Cumberland Plateau.
36. Deyle, *Carry Me Back*, 205–07.
37. Egerton, *Visions Utopia*.
38. Manning, *Historic Cumberland Plateau*, 265–68.
39. *Two Years in Harriman*.
40. Manning, *Historic Cumberland Plateau*, 150–51.
41. Ibid., 246–51.

CONCLUSION

1. Dudney, *Sons of the Cumberland*, 6–8.
2. John Duncan Sr.'s father was Flem B. Duncan, son of Emanuel Duncan. Emanuel's father was Henry Duncan and lived just north of Huntsville. See "The Thomas Family of Scott County, Tennessee," in *FNB Chronicles*, compiled by Louise Carson, September 6, 2008.

BIBLIOGRAPHY

Abernethy, Thomas. *From Frontier to Plantation in Tennessee: A Study in Frontier Democracy*. Chapel Hill: University of North Carolina Press, 1932.

Arbuckle, J.W. *Cowan Pusher District and Tunnel*. Winchester, TN: Herald-Chronicle, 1994.

Aron, Stephen. *How the West Was Lost: The Transformation of Kentucky from Daniel Boone to Henry Clay*. Baltimore: Johns Hopkins University Press, 1999.

Ash, Stephen V. *Middle Tennessee Society Transformed, 1860–1870: War and Peace in the Upper South*. Knoxville: University of Tennessee Press, 2006.

Astor, Aaron. *Rebels on the Border: Civil War, Emancipation, and the Reconstruction of Kentucky and Missouri*. Baton Rouge: Louisiana State University Press, 2012.

Atkins, Jonathan M. *Parties, Politics, and the Sectional Conflict in Tennessee, 1832–1861*. 1st ed. Knoxville: University of Tennessee Press, 1997.

Baggett, James Alex. *Homegrown Yankees: Tennessee's Union Cavalry in the Civil War*. Baton Rouge: Louisiana State University Press, 2009.

Banker, Mark T. *Appalachians All: East Tennesseans and the Elusive History of an American Region*. 1st ed. Knoxville: University of Tennessee Press, 2011.

Baptist, Edward E. *The Half Has Never Been Told: Slavery and the Making of American Capitalism*. New York: Basic Books, 2014.

Barksdale, Kevin T. *The Lost State of Franklin: America's First Secession*. Lexington: University Press of Kentucky, 2010.

Bergeron, Paul H., Jeannette Keith and Stephen V. Ash. *Tennesseans & Their History*. Knoxville: University of Tennessee Press, 1999.

Berlin, Ira, Joseph P. Reidy and Leslie S. Rowland, eds. *Freedom: Series II: The Black Military Experience: A Documentary History of Emancipation, 1861–1867.* New York: Cambridge University Press, 1983.

Biggers, Jeff. *The United States of Appalachia: How Southern Mountaineers Brought Independence, Culture, and Enlightenment to America.* Emeryville, CA: Counterpoint, 2007. Lexington: University Press of Kentucky, 2009.

Blackmon, Douglas A. *Slavery by Another Name: The Re-Enslavement of Black Americans from the Civil War to World War II.* Reprint ed. New York: Anchor, 2009.

Blankenship, Amanda McDowell. *Fiddles in the Cumberlands.* New York: Richard R. Smith, 1943.

Blevins, Jerry. *Sequatchie Valley Soldiers in the Civil War: Bledsoe, Grundy, Marion, and Sequatchie Counties in Tennessee and Jackson County in Alabama.* N.p.: J. Blevins, 1990.

Bradley, Michael R. *Tullahoma: The 1863 Campaign for the Control of Middle Tennessee.* Shippensburg, PA: White Mane Publishing Company, 1999.

Brents, J. *The Patriots and Guerillas of East Tennessee and Kentucky.* New York: Henry Dexter, 1863.

Brooks, Maurice. *The Appalachians.* Boston: Houghton Mifflin Company, 1965.

Bryson, Bill. *A Short History of Nearly Everything.* 1st ed. Westport, CT: Broadway Books, 2004.

Bullard, Helen. *Cumberland County's First Hundred Years.* 1st ed. N.p.: Centennial Committee, 1956.

Byerly, Don W. *The Last Billion Years: A Geologic History of Tennessee.* 1st ed. Knoxville: University of Tennessee Press, 2013.

Campbell, Mary Emily Robertson. *The Attitude of Tennesseans toward the Union, 1847–1861.* New York: Vantage Press, 1961.

Caruso, John Anthony. *The Appalachian Frontier: America's First Surge Westward.* New York: Bobbs Merrill, 1959.

Caudill, Harry M., and Stewart L. Udall. *Night Comes to the Cumberlands: A Biography of a Depressed Area.* Boston: Little, Brown and Company, 1963.

Christian, David, and William H. McNeill. *Maps of Time: An Introduction to Big History.* Berkeley: University of California Press, 2011.

Cimprich, John. *Slavery's End in Tennessee.* 1st ed. Tuscaloosa: University of Alabama Press, 2002.

"Civil War Data." American Civil War Research Database. http://www.civilwardata.com/active/index.html (accessed December 23, 2014).

"Compiled Service Records." Fold3. http://www.fold3.com (accessed December 23, 2014).

Connelly, Thomas Lawrence. *Army of the Heartland: The Army of Tennessee, 1861–1862.* Baton Rouge: Louisiana State University Press, 2001.

———. *Autumn of Glory: The Army of Tennessee, 1862–1865.* Baton Rouge: Louisiana State University Press, 2001.

Cowles, Calvin D. *Atlas to Accompany the Official Records of the Union and Confederate Armies.* Washington, D.C.: Government Printing Office, 1891–1895.

Cozzens, Peter. *No Better Place to Die: The Battle of Stones River.* Urbana: University of Illinois Press, 1991.

———. *The Shipwreck of Their Hopes: The Battles for Chattanooga.* 1st ed. Urbana: University of Illinois Press, 1996.

———. *This Terrible Sound: The Battle of Chickamauga.* Urbana: University of Illinois Press, 1996.

Crawford, Martin. *Ashe County's Civil War: Community and Society in the Appalachian South.* 1st ed. Charlottesville: University of Virginia Press, 2001.

Crofts, Daniel W. *Reluctant Confederates: Upper South Unionists in the Secession Crisis.* Reprint ed. Chapel Hill: University of North Carolina Press, 1988.

Daniel, Larry J. *Days of Glory: The Army of the Cumberland, 1861–1865.* Baton Rouge: Louisiana State University Press, 2004.

DeLorme. *Tennessee Atlas & Gazetteer.* 9th ed. Yarmouth, ME: DeLorme Publishing, 2010.

Deyle, Steven. *Carry Me Back: The Domestic Slave Trade in American Life.* Oxford, UK: Oxford University Press, 2005.

Dickinson, W. Calvin. *Morgan County.* Memphis, TN: Memphis State University Press, 1987.

———. "The Walton Road." *Tennessee Anthropologist* 20, no. 2 (Fall 1995): 126–37.

Dillard, John Roy. *Standing Stone, Tenn. Monterey: Early History.* 1st ed. Nashville, TN: Harris Press, 1989.

Drake, Doug. *Founding of the Cumberland Settlements.* 2nd ed. Gallatin, TN: Warioto Press, 2009.

Dudney, Betty Jane. "The Civil War in White County, Tennessee, 1861–1865." Master's thesis, Tennessee Technological University, 1985.

Dudney, Mark. *Sons of the Cumberland: The Early Years of Cordell Hull and John Jordan Gore.* Sparta, WI: AuthorHouse, 2012.

Dunigan, Tom. "Tennessee Landforms." Tennessee Landforms, December 12, 2014. http://tnlandforms.us/landforms.

Dunn, Durwood. *Cades Cove: The Life and Death of a Southern Appalachian Community, 1818–1937.* 1st ed. Knoxville: University of Tennessee Press, 1988.

———. *The Civil War in Southern Appalachian Methodism.* Knoxville: University of Tennessee Press, 2014.

Efford, Alison Clark. *German Immigrants, Race, and Citizenship in the Civil War Era.* Cambridge, UK: Cambridge University Press, 2013.

Egerton, John. *Visions Utopia: Nashoba, Rugby, Ruskin, New Communities.* 1st ed. Knoxville: University of Tennessee Press, 1977.

"Eighth Population Census Manuscripts—1860." Ancestry.com. http://home.ancestry.com (accessed December 23, 2014).

"Eighth Slave Census Manuscripts—1860." Ancestry.com. http://home.ancestry.com (accessed December 23, 2014).

Einolf, Christopher J. *George Thomas: Virginian for the Union.* Norman: University of Oklahoma Press, 2010.

Elliott, Sam Davis. *Isham G. Harris of Tennessee: Confederate Governor and United States Senator.* 1st ed. Baton Rouge: Louisiana State University Press, 2010.

Ellis, Daniel. *The Thrilling Adventures of Daniel Ellis: The Great Union Guide of East Tennessee for a Period of Nearly Four Years During the Great Southern Rebellion.* New York: Harper and Brothers, 1867.

Fellman, Michael. *Inside War: The Guerrilla Conflict in Missouri during the American Civil War.* New York: Oxford University Press, 1989.

Fisher, Noel C. *War at Every Door: Partisan Politics and Guerrilla Violence in East Tennessee, 1860–1869.* Chapel Hill: University of North Carolina Press, 2001.

Glen, John M. *Highlander: No Ordinary School.* 2nd ed. Knoxville: University of Tennessee Press, 1996.

Goodspeed, Westin A. *History of Tennessee: From the Earliest Time to the Present, Cannon, Coffee, DeKalb, Warren, White Counties of Tennessee.* Nashville, TN: Goodspeed Publishing Company, 1887.

———. *History of Tennessee Illustrated: 30 East Tennessee Counties.* Nashville, TN: Goodspeed Publishing Company, 1887.

Groce, W. Todd. *Mountain Rebels: East Tennessee Confederates, 1860–1870.* 1st ed. Knoxville: University of Tennessee Press, 2000.

Hafendorfer, Kenneth A. *The Battle of Wild Cat Mountain.* 1st ed. Louisville, KY: KH Press, 2003.

Hannah, Howard. *Confederate Action in Franklin County, Tennessee.* Sewanee, TN: University Press, 1963.

Hardy, William E. "'Fare Well to All Radicals': Redeeming Tennessee, 1869–1870." University of Tennessee, 2013.

Harrison, Lowell H. *The Civil War in Kentucky.* 1st ed. Lexington: University Press of Kentucky, 2009.

Harvey, Stella Mowbray. *Tales of the Civil War Era*. Crossville, TN: Chronicle Publishing Company, 1963.

Hess, Earl J. *Banners to the Breeze: The Kentucky Campaign, Corinth, and Stones River*. Lincoln: University of Nebraska Press, 2010.

———. *The Civil War in the West: Victory and Defeat from the Appalachians to the Mississippi*. Book Club ed. Chapel Hill: University of North Carolina Press, 2012.

———. *The Knoxville Campaign: Burnside and Longstreet in East Tennessee*. 1st ed. Knoxville: University of Tennessee Press, 2013.

Hogue, Albert Ross. *History of Fentress County, Tennessee: The Old Home of Mark Twain's Ancestors*. World War Memorial ed., 1920. Baltimore, MD: RPC, 2002.

———. *Mark Twain's Obedstown*. Jamestown, VA: Fentress County Historical Society, reprinted 1990.

Houk, Rose. *Great Smoky Mountains: A Natural History Guide*. Boston: Mariner Books, 1993.

Hsiung, David C. *Two Worlds in the Tennessee Mountains: Exploring the Origins of Appalachian Stereotypes*. Lexington: University Press of Kentucky, 2014.

Hurst, Jack. *Nathan Bedford Forrest: A Biography*. Reprint ed. New York: Vintage, 1994.

Hutton, T.R.C. *Bloody Breathitt: Politics and Violence in the Appalachian South*. Lexington: University Press of Kentucky, 2013.

Inscoe, John C., ed. *Appalachians and Race: The Mountain South from Slavery to Segregation*. Lexington: University Press of Kentucky, 2005.

———. *Mountain Masters: Slavery Sectional Crisis Western North Carolina*. Knoxville: University of Tennessee Press, 1996.

Inscoe, John C., and Gordon B. McKinney. *The Heart of Confederate Appalachia: Western North Carolina in the Civil War*. 1st ed. Chapel Hill: University of North Carolina Press, 2000.

Johnson, Andrew. *The Papers of Andrew Johnson*. Vol. 4: 1860–1861. Edited by Leroy P. Graf and Ralph W. Haskins. Knoxville: University of Tennessee Press, 1976.

———. *The Papers of Andrew Johnson*. Vol. 6, 1862–1864. Edited by Leroy P. Graf and Ralph W. Haskins. Knoxville: University of Tennessee Press, 1983.

Jones, Evan C. *Gateway to the Confederacy: New Perspectives on the Chickamauga and Chattanooga Campaigns, 1862–1863*. Edited by Wiley Sword. Baton Rouge: Louisiana State University Press, 2014.

Jones, William. "The Civil War in Van Buren County, 1861–1865." *Tennessee Historical Quarterly* 67 (Spring 2008): 56–64.

Kazin, Michael. *A Godly Hero: The Life of William Jennings Bryan*. New York: Anchor, 2007.

Kenny, Kevin. *Peaceable Kingdom Lost: The Paxton Boys and the Destruction of William Penn's Holy Experiment.* 1st ed. New York: Oxford University Press, 2011.

Kenzer, Robert C. *Kinship and Neighborhood in a Southern Community: Orange County, North Carolina, 1849–1881.* 1st ed. Knoxville: University of Tennessee Press, 1988.

Killebrew, Joseph Buckner. *Tennessee: Its Agricultural and Mineral Wealth.* Nashville, TN: Tavel, Eastman and Howell, 1876.

Larson, Edward J. *Summer for the Gods: The Scopes Trial and America's Continuing Debate Over Science and Religion*. First trade paper ed. New York: Basic Books, 2006.

Luther, Edward T. *Our Restless Earth: Geologic Regions Tennessee.* 1st ed. Knoxville: University of Tennessee Press, 1977.

Mackey, Robert Russell. *The Uncivil War: Irregular Warfare in the Upper South, 1861–1865.* 1st ed. Norman: University of Oklahoma Press, 2004.

Manning, Russ. *40 Hikes in Tennessee's South Cumberland.* 3rd ed. Seattle, WA: Mountaineers Books, 2000.

———. *Historic Cumberland Plateau.* 2nd ed. Knoxville: University of Tennessee Press, 1999.

———. *100 Trails of the Big South Fork: Tennessee and Kentucky.* 4th ed. Seattle, WA: Mountaineers Books, 2000.

Matthews, Larry E. *Big Bone Cave.* Huntsville, AL: National Speleological Society, 2006.

Mays, Thomas D. *Cumberland Blood: Champ Ferguson's Civil War.* 1st ed. Carbondale: Southern Illinois University Press, 2008.

McCurry, Stephanie. *Masters of Small Worlds: Yeoman Households, Gender Relations, and the Political Culture of the Antebellum South Carolina Low Country.* New York: Oxford University Press, 1997.

McDade, Arthur. *Natural Arches Big South Fork: Guide to Selected Landforms.* Knoxville: University of Tennessee Press, 2000.

McDonough, James Lee. *Shiloh—In Hell before Night.* 1st ed. Knoxville: University of Tennessee Press, 1977.

———. *War in Kentucky: Shiloh to Perryville.* 1st ed. Knoxville: University of Tennessee Press, 1994.

McKenzie, Robert Tracy. *Lincolnites and Rebels: A Divided Town in Civil War America.* New York: Oxford University Press, 2009.

———. *One South or Many?: Plantation Belt and Upcountry in Civil War–Era Tennessee.* Cambridge, UK: Cambridge University Press, 2002.

McKinney, Gordon B. *Reconstructing Appalachia: The Civil War's Aftermath.* Edited by Andrew L. Slap. Reprint ed. Lexington: University Press of Kentucky, 2014.

McKnight, Brian. *Confederate Outlaw: Champ Ferguson and the Civil War in Appalachia.* Baton Rouge: Louisiana State University Press, 2011.

Miller, Gregory. *The Civil War and Campbell County, Tennessee.* Jacksboro, TX: Lafollette Press, 1992.

Miller, Ralph L. "Where and Why of Pine Mountain and Other Major Fault Planes, Virginia, Kentucky and Tennessee." *American Journal of Science* 273-A (1973): 353–71.

Molloy, Johnny. *Explorer's Guide 50 Hikes on Tennessee's Cumberland Plateau: Walks, Hikes, and Backpacks from the Tennessee River Gorge to the Big South Fork and throughout the Cumberlands.* 1st ed. New York: Countryman Press, 2012.

Montell, William Lynwood. *Don't Go Up Kettle Creek: Verbal Legacy of the Upper Cumberland.* Knoxville: University of Tennessee Press, 2000.

Moore, Harry L. *Geologic Trip Across Tennessee: Interstate 40.* Knoxville: University of Tennessee Press, 1994.

Muir, John, and Peter Jenkins. *A Thousand-Mile Walk to the Gulf.* Boston: Mariner Books, 1998.

Noe, Kenneth W. *Perryville: This Grand Havoc of Battle.* 1st ed. Lexington: University Press of Kentucky, 2001.

———. *Southwest Virginia's Railroad: Modernization and the Sectional Crisis in the Civil War Era.* Tuscaloosa: University of Alabama Press, 2003.

Noe, Kenneth W., and Shannon H. Wilson, eds. *The Civil War in Appalachia: Collected Essays.* Knoxville: University of Tennessee Press, 2004.

Oakes, James. *Freedom National: The Destruction of Slavery in the United States, 1861–1865.* 1st ed. New York: W.W. Norton & Company, 2012.

Ogle, George. *Biographies of the Cumberland Region of Tennessee.* Reprint of the 1898 original. Joplin, MO: Hearthstone Legacy Publications, 2010.

O'Neal, Mike. "The Civil War on the Upper Cumberland Plateau in Tennessee." *Scott County Historical Society Newsletter* (Winter/Spring 1986).

Ott, Ethel Freytag, and Glena Kreis. *A History of Morgan County, Tennessee.* Wartburg, IA: Specialty Printing Company, 1971.

Plemons, Douglas. "The United States Saltpeter Cave Survey, 2006." *Journal of Spelean History* 41.2, no. 132 (December 2007).

Powell, David. *The Chickamauga Campaign—A Mad Irregular Battle: From the Crossing of Tennessee River Through the Second Day, August 22–September 19, 1863.* El Dorado Hills, CA: Savas Beatie, 2014.

Ramage, James A. *Rebel Raider: The Life of General John Hunt Morgan.* Reissue ed. Lexington: University Press of Kentucky, 1995.

Ramage, James A., and Andrea S. Watkins. *Kentucky Rising: Democracy, Slavery, and Culture from the Early Republic to the Civil War.* Book Club ed. Lexington: University Press of Kentucky, 2011.

Raulston, J. Leonard, and James Weston Livingood. *Sequatchie: A Story of the Southern Cumberlands.* Knoxville: University of Tennessee Press, 1974.

Ray, Kristofer. *Middle Tennessee, 1775–1825: Progress and Popular Democracy on the Southwestern Frontier.* 1st ed. Knoxville: University of Tennessee Press, 2007.

Robinson, Armstead L., Joseph P. Reidy and Barbara J. Fields. *Bitter Fruits of Bondage: The Demise of Slavery and the Collapse of the Confederacy, 1861–1865.* Charlottesville: University of Virginia Press, 2004.

Robnett, Elizabeth Parham. *Bledsoe County, Tennessee: A History.* 1st ed. Pikeville, TN: Mountain Press, 1993.

Roy, Paul. *Scott County in the Civil War.* Huntsville, TN: Scott County Historical Society, 2001.

Ryder, Robert T. "Cincinnati Arch Province." *U.S. Geological Survey* no. 66 (n.d.).

Safford, James M. *Geology of Tennessee.* Nashville, TN: S.C. Mercer, 1869.

Sanderson, Esther Sharp. *County Scott and Its Mountain Folk.* 1st ed. Huntsville, TN: Blue and Gray Press, 1958.

Sanders, Stuart W. *The Battle of Mill Springs, Kentucky.* Charleston, SC: The History Press, 2013.

Sarris, Jonathan Dean. *A Separate Civil War: Communities in Conflict in the Mountain South.* Charlottesville: University of Virginia Press, 2012.

Schroeder, Albert, ed. "Writings of a Tennessee Unionist." *Tennessee Historical Quarterly* 9 (September 1950): 244–72.

Severance, Dr. Ben H. *Tennessee's Radical Army: The State Guard and Its Role in Reconstruction, 1867–1869.* 1st ed. Knoxville: University of Tennessee Press, 2005.

Shapiro, Karin A. *A New South Rebellion: The Battle against Convict Labor in the Tennessee Coalfields, 1871–1896.* Chapel Hill: University of North Carolina Press, 1998.

Siburt, James T. "Colonel John Hughs: Brigade Commander and Confederate Guerrilla." *Tennessee Historical Quarterly* 51, no. 2 (1992): 87–95.

Smith, Marion. "In Quest of a Supply of Saltpeter in Early Civil War Tennessee." *Tennessee Historical Quarterly* 61, no. 2 (2002): 96–111.

Sutherland, Daniel E. *A Savage Conflict: The Decisive Role of Guerrillas in the American Civil War.* 1st ed. Chapel Hill: University of North Carolina Press, 2013.

Tarrant, E. *The Wild Riders of the First Kentucky Cavalry: A History of the Regiment in the War of the Rebellion, 1861–1865*. Louisville, KY: R.H. Carothers, 1894.

Temple, Oliver. *Notable Men of Tennessee: From 1833 to 1875*. New York: Cosmopolitan Press, 1912.

"Tennessee and the Civil War." http://www.tngenweb.org/civilwar (accessed December 23, 2014).

"Tennessee Cave Survey." http://www.subworks.com/tcs (accessed December 24, 2014).

Tennessee Historical Commission. *Tennesseans in the Civil War: Part 2; A Military History of Confederate and Union Units with Available Rosters of Personnel*. Nashville: Civil War Centennial Commission of Tennessee, 1965.

Two Years in Harriman, Tennessee. New York: South Publishing Company, 1892.

Wade, Gregory L. *Broken Valley: A Wartime Story of Isolation, Fear and Hope in a Remote East Tennessee Valley*. Bloomington, IN: iUniverse, 2014.

Walter, Bill, and Larry E. Matthews. *Blue Spring Cave*. Edited by G. Tom Rea. 1st ed. Huntsville, AL: National Speleological Society, 2010.

The War of the Rebellion: A Compilation of the Official Records of the Union and Confederate Armies. Washington, D.C.: Government Printing Office, 1880–1901.

Wegener, Alfred. *The Origin of Continents and Oceans*. Reprint and English translation. New York: Dover Publications, 2011.

Whiteaker, Larry. "Battle of Dug Hill: A Bloody Mystery." *Cookeville Herald-Citizen*, March 7, 2010, C8.

Whites, LeeAnn. "Forty Shirts and a Wagonload of Wheat: Women, the Domestic Supply Line, and the Civil War on the Western Border." *Journal of the Civil War Era* 1, no. 1 (2011): 56–78.

White, William Lee. *Bushwhacking on a Grand Scale: The Battle of Chickamauga, September 18–20, 1863*. El Dorado Hills, CA: Savas Beatie, 2013.

Wiley, Martha Evans. *Cumberland Gap National Historical Park*. Charleston, SC: Arcadia Publishing, 2014.

Williams, John Alexander. *Appalachia: A History*. Chapel Hill: University of North Carolina Press, 2002.

Wills, Brian Steel. *George Henry Thomas: As True as Steel*. 1st ed. Lawrence: University Press of Kansas, 2012.

Wirt, Alvin B. *The Upper Cumberland of Pioneer Times*. Washington, D.C.: Alvin Wirt, 1954.

Woodworth, Steven E. *Six Armies in Tennessee: The Chickamauga and Chattanooga Campaigns*. Lincoln, NE: Bison Books, 1999.

Wright, A.B. *Autobiography of Rev. A.B. Wright, of the Holston Conference, M.E. Church*. London: Fentress County Historical Society, 1977.

Index

ABOUT THE AUTHOR

Aaron Astor, PhD, is associate professor of history at Maryville College in Maryville, Tennessee. He has written numerous articles, conference papers and book chapters on the Civil War era, focusing especially on the Upper and Border South. He is the author of the book *Rebels on the Border: Civil War, Emancipation, and the Reconstruction of Kentucky and Missouri, 1860–1872*, published by LSU Press for its Conflicting Worlds: New Perspectives on the Civil War series. The book, which examines the transformation of grass-roots black and white politics in the Border South, developed as a revision of his dissertation completed under the direction of Pulitzer Prize runner-up Stephanie McCurry and Pulitzer winner Steven Hahn, both now at the University of Pennsylvania. He has also written eleven articles for the award-winning *New York Times* Disunion series, addressing such topics as guerrilla warfare; battles and campaigns in the western theater and Tennessee; popular politics; emancipation and race; and regional identity in the Appalachian South.

Dr. Astor teaches at Maryville College, a private liberal arts college in Tennessee, where he covers a wide range of topics in American history from the Revolution to the present. He contributes to several Civil War preservation and public education organizations in Tennessee and regularly speaks about the Civil War and regional identity in the Upper South. He is currently the president of the East Tennessee Civil War Alliance. He serves on the Tennessee Civil War Preservation Association Board. He also serves on the membership committees of the Southern Historical Association and the Society of Civil War Historians.

Dr. Astor graduated from Hamilton College in 1995 with a bachelor's degree in philosophy. Astor then entered Northwestern University, where he earned his master's degree in 2001 and PhD in history in 2006. He has taught at Maryville College since 2007.

Aaron Astor lives in Maryville, Tennessee, with his wife, Samantha; his three sons, Henry, Teddy and Jimmy; and his twin daughters, Lillian and Sadie.

Printed in the USA
CPSIA information can be obtained
at www.ICGtesting.com
LVHW010724281123
765137LV00006B/70